Cisco 200-301 CCNA

Pass your CISCO CCNA (Cisco Certified Network Associate) 200-301 Certification on your first try.

The exam's duration is 120 minutes and you can expect about 100-120 questions.

This New Book contains 2 complete Exclusive and new practice tests, of 120 questions each, just like you will get in the official exam.

So, this new book contains over 240 new and exclusive questions to see how prepared you are for the real test.

This book is a great way to assess your readiness, and discover your weakness areas.

The exams were compiled by Experts team whom have all passed the official exams. This new preparation book covers all the exam domains.

The practice tests are formatted just like the real official exam questions would be.

We're confident that you will easily pass your CISCO CCNA 200-301 after taking these practice exams.

We are looking forward to seeing you in the preparation book.

Practice Test I

1)

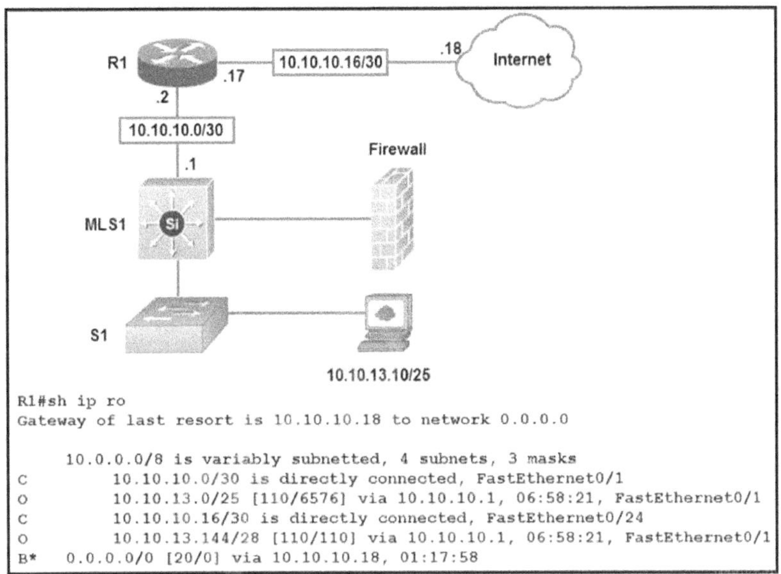


```
R1#sh ip ro
Gateway of last resort is 10.10.10.18 to network 0.0.0.0

     10.0.0.0/8 is variably subnetted, 4 subnets, 3 masks
C        10.10.10.0/30 is directly connected, FastEthernet0/1
O        10.10.13.0/25 [110/6576] via 10.10.10.1, 06:58:21, FastEthernet0/1
C        10.10.10.16/30 is directly connected, FastEthernet0/24
O        10.10.13.144/28 [110/110] via 10.10.10.1, 06:58:21, FastEthernet0/1
B*   0.0.0.0/0 [20/0] via 10.10.10.18, 01:17:58
```

Refer to the exhibit. Which type of route does R1 use to reach host 10.10.13.10/32?

A. default route

B. network route

C. host route

D. floating static route

2)

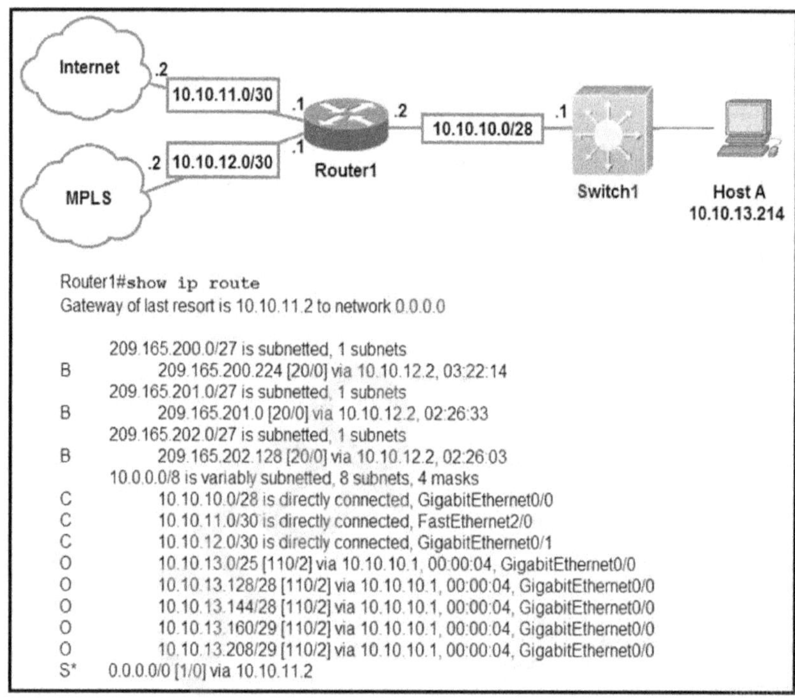


```
Router1#show ip route
Gateway of last resort is 10.10.11.2 to network 0.0.0.0

        209.165.200.0/27 is subnetted, 1 subnets
B           209.165.200.224 [20/0] via 10.10.12.2, 03:22:14
        209.165.201.0/27 is subnetted, 1 subnets
B           209.165.201.0 [20/0] via 10.10.12.2, 02:26:33
        209.165.202.0/27 is subnetted, 1 subnets
B           209.165.202.128 [20/0] via 10.10.12.2, 02:26:03
        10.0.0.0/8 is variably subnetted, 8 subnets, 4 masks
C           10.10.10.0/28 is directly connected, GigabitEthernet0/0
C           10.10.11.0/30 is directly connected, FastEthernet2/0
C           10.10.12.0/30 is directly connected, GigabitEthernet0/1
O           10.10.13.0/25 [110/2] via 10.10.10.1, 00:00:04, GigabitEthernet0/0
O           10.10.13.128/28 [110/2] via 10.10.10.1, 00:00:04, GigabitEthernet0/0
O           10.10.13.144/28 [110/2] via 10.10.10.1, 00:00:04, GigabitEthernet0/0
O           10.10.13.160/29 [110/2] via 10.10.10.1, 00:00:04, GigabitEthernet0/0
O           10.10.13.208/29 [110/2] via 10.10.10.1, 00:00:04, GigabitEthernet0/0
S*      0.0.0.0/0 [1/0] via 10.10.11.2
```

Refer to the exhibit. Which prefix does Router1 use for traffic to Host A?

A. 10.10.10.0/28

B. 10.10.13.0/25

C. 10.10.13.144/28

D. 10.10.13.208/29

3) A frame that enters a switch fails the Frame Check Sequence. Which two interface counters are incremented? (Choose two.)

A. input errors

B. frame

C. giants

D. CRC

E. runts

4) How do TCP and UDP differ in the way that they establish a connection between two endpoints?

A. TCP uses the three-way handshake, and UDP does not guarantee message delivery.

B. TCP uses synchronization packets, and UDP uses acknowledgment packets.

C. UDP provides reliable message transfer, and TCP is a connectionless protocol.

D. UDP uses SYN, SYN ACK, and FIN bits in the frame header while TCP uses SYN, SYN ACK, and ACK bits.

5) Which 802.11 frame type is Association Response?

A. management.

B. protected frame.

C. action.

D. control.

6) In which way does a spine-and-leaf architecture allow for scalability in a network when additional access ports are required?

A. A spine switch and a leaf switch can be added with redundant connections between them.

B. A spine switch can be added with at least 40 GB uplinks.

C. A leaf switch can be added with connections to every spine switch.

D. A leaf switch can be added with a single connection to a core spine switch.

7) What identifies the functionality of virtual machines?

A. The hypervisor communicates on Layer 3 without the need for additional resources.

B. Each hypervisor supports a single virtual machine and a single software switch.

C. The hypervisor virtualizes physical components including CPU, memory, and storage.

D. Virtualized servers run efficiently when physically connected to a switch that is separate from the hypervisor.

8) Which command automatically generates an IPv6 address from a specified IPv6 prefix and MAC address of an interface?

A. ipv6 address dhcp

B. ipv6 address 2001:DB8:5:112::/64 eui-64

C. ipv6 address autoconfig

D. ipv6 address 2001:DB8:5:112::2/64 link-local

9) What is the default behavior of a Layer 2 switch when a frame with an unknown destination MAC address is received?

A. The Layer 2 switch forwards the packet and adds the destination MAC address to its MAC address table.

B. The Layer 2 switch sends a copy of a packet to CPU for destination MAC address learning.

C. The Layer 2 switch floods packets to all ports except the receiving port in the given VLAN.

D. The Layer 2 switch drops the received frame.

10) An engineer must configure a /30 subnet between two routes. Which usable IP address and subnet mask combination meets this criteria?

A. interface e0/0 description to XX-AXXX:XXXXX ip address 10.2.1.3 255.255.255.252

B. interface e0/0 description to XX-AXXX:XXXXX ip address 192.168.1.1 255.255.255.248

C. interface e0/0 description to XX-AXXX:XXXXX ip address 172.16.1.4 255.255.255.248

D. interface e0/0 description to XX-AXXX:XXXXX ip address 209.165.201.2 225.255.255.252

11) Which network allows devices to communicate without the need to access the Internet?

A. 172.9.0.0/16

B. 172.28.0.0/16

C. 192.0.0.0/8

D. 209.165.201.0/24

12)

```
Router(config)#interface GigabitEthernet 1/0/1
Router(config-if)#ip address 192.168.16.143 255.255.255.240
Bad mask /28 for address 192.168.16.143
```

Refer to the exhibit. Which statement explains the configuration error message that is received?

A. It belongs to a private IP address range.

B. The router does not support /28 mask.

C. It is a network IP address.

D. It is a broadcast IP address.

13) Which IPv6 address type provides communication between subnets and cannot route on the Internet?

A. link-local

B. unique local

C. multicast

D. global unicast

14) Which IPv6 address block sends packets to a group address rather than a single address?

A. 2000::/3

B. FC00::/7

C. FE80::/10

D. FF00::/8

15) What are two reasons that cause late collisions to increment on an Ethernet interface? (Choose two.)

A. when Carrier Sense Multiple Access/Collision Detection is used.

B. when one side of the connection is configured for half-duplex.

C. when the sending device waits 15 seconds before sending the frame again.

D. when a collision occurs after the 32nd byte of a frame has been transmitted.

E. when the cable length limits are exceeded.

16) What is a benefit of using a Cisco Wireless LAN Controller?

A. It eliminates the need to configure each access point individually.

B. Central AP management requires more complex configurations.

C. Unique SSIDs cannot use the same authentication method.

D. It supports autonomous and lightweight APs.

17) Which action is taken by switch port enabled for PoE power classification override?

A. If a monitored port exceeds the maximum administrative value for power, the port is shut down and err-disabled.

B. When a powered device begins drawing power from a PoE switch port, a syslog message is generated.

C. As power usage on a PoE switch port is checked, data flow to the connected device is temporarily paused.

D. If a switch determines that a device is using less than the minimum configured power, it assumes the device has failed and disconnects it.

18) What occurs to frames during the process of frame flooding?

A. Frames are sent to all ports, including those that are assigned to other VLANs.

B. Frames are sent to every port on the switch that has a matching entry in MAC address table.

C. Frames are sent to every port on the switch in the same VLAN except from the originating port.

D. Frames are sent to every port on the switch in the same VLAN.

19) Which function does the range of private IPv4 addresses perform?

A. allows multiple companies to each use the same addresses without conflicts.

B. provides a direct connection for hosts from outside of the enterprise network.

C. ensures that NAT is not required to reach the Internet with private range addressing.

D. enables secure communications to the Internet for all external hosts.

20) Which action must be taken to assign a global unicast IPv6 address on an interface that is derived from the MAC address of that interface?

A. explicitly assign a link-local address.

B. disable the EUI-64 bit process.

C. enable SLAAC on an interface.

D. configure a stateful DHCPv6 server on the network.

21) Several new coverage cells are required to improve the Wi-Fi network of an organization. Which two standard designs are recommended? (Choose two.)

A. 5GHz provides increased network capacity with up to 23 nonoverlapping channels.

B. 5GHz channel selection requires an autonomous access point.

C. Cells that overlap one another are configured to use nonoverlapping channels.

D. Adjacent cells with overlapping channels use a repeater access point.

E. For maximum throughput, the WLC is configured to dynamically set adjacent access points to the channel.

22) How do TCP and UDP differ in the way they provide reliability for delivery of packets?

A. TCP does not guarantee delivery or error checking to ensure that there is no corruption of data, UDP provides message acknowledgement and retransmits data if lost.

B. TCP provides flow control to avoid overwhelming a receiver by sending too many packets at once, UDP sends packets to the receiver in a continuous stream without checking.

C. TCP is a connectionless protocol that does not provide reliable delivery of data; UDP is a connection-oriented protocol that uses sequencing to provide reliable delivery.

D. TCP uses windowing to deliver packets reliably; UDP provides reliable message transfer between hosts by establishing a three-way handshake.

23) What are two differences between optical-fiber cabling and copper cabling? (Choose two.)

A. A BNC connector is used for fiber connections.

B. The glass core component is encased in a cladding.

C. The data can pass through the cladding.

D. Light is transmitted through the core of the fiber.

E. Fiber connects to physical interfaces using RJ-45 connections.

24) How does CAPWAP communicate between an access point in local mode and a WLC?

A. The access point must not be connected to the wired network, as it would create a loop.

B. The access point must be connected to the same switch as the WLC.

C. The access point must directly connect to the WLC using a copper cable.

D. The access point has the ability to link to any switch in the network, assuming connectivity to the WLC.

25) Which IPv6 address block forwards packets to a multicast address rather than a unicast address?

A. 2000::/3

B. FC00::/7

C. FE80::/10

D. FF00::/12

26) What is the difference regarding reliability and communication type between TCP and UDP?

A. TCP is reliable and is a connectionless protocol; UDP is not reliable and is a connection-oriented protocol.

B. TCP is not reliable and is a connectionless protocol; UDP is reliable and is a connection-oriented protocol.

C. TCP is not reliable and is a connection-oriented protocol; UDP is reliable and is a connectionless protocol.

D. TCP is reliable and is a connection-oriented protocol; UDP is not reliable and is a connectionless protocol.

27) What are two descriptions of three-tier network topologies? (Choose two.)

A. The distribution layer runs Layer 2 and Layer 3 technologies.

B. The network core is designed to maintain continuous connectivity when devices fail.

C. The access layer manages routing between devices in different domains.

D. The core layer maintains wired connections for each host.

E. The core and distribution layers perform the same functions.

28) Which type of IPv6 address is publicly routable in the same way as IPv4 public addresses?

A. multicast.

B. unique local.

C. link-local.

D. global unicast.

29) What is the expected outcome when an EUI-64 address is generated?

A. The interface ID is configured as a random 64-bit value.

B. The characters FE80 are inserted at the beginning of the MAC address of the interface.

C. The seventh bit of the original MAC address of the interface is inverted.

D. The MAC address of the interface is used as the interface ID without modification.

30) A corporate office uses four floors in a building.

☞ **Floor 1 has 24 users.**

☞ **Floor 2 has 29 users.**

☞ **Floor 3 has 28 users.**

Floor 4 has 22 users.

Which subnet summarizes and gives the most efficient distribution of IP addresses for the router configuration?

A.   192.168.0.0/24   as   summary   and 192.168.0.0/28 for each floor.

B.   192.168.0.0/23   as   summary   and 192.168.0.0/25 for each floor.

C.   192.168.0.0/25   as   summary   and 192.168.0.0/27 for each floor.

D.   192.168.0.0/26   as   summary   and 192.168.0.0/29 for each floor.

31)

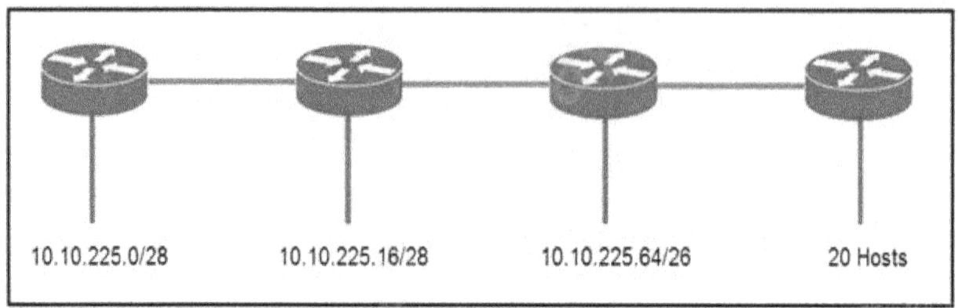

Refer to the exhibit. An engineer must add a subnet for a new office that will add 20 users to the network. Which IPv4 network and subnet mask combination does the engineer assign to minimize wasting addresses?

A. 10.10.225.48 255.255.255.240

B. 10.10.225.32 255.255.255.240

C. 10.10.225.48 255.255.255.224

D. 10.10.225.32 255.255.255.224

32) What is a characteristic of spine-and-leaf architecture?

A. Each link between leaf switches allows for higher bandwidth.

B. It provides greater predictability on STP blocked ports.

C. It provides variable latency.

D. Each device is separated by the same number of hops.

33) An office has 8 floors with approximately 30-40 users per floor. One subnet must be used. Which command must be configured on the router Switched Virtual Interface to use address space efficiently?

A. ip address 192.168.0.0 255.255.0.0

B. ip address 192.168.0.0 255.255.254.0

C. ip address 192.168.0.0 255.255.255.128

D. ip address 192.168.0.0 255.255.255.224

34) A device detects two stations transmitting frames at the same time. This condition occurs after the first 64 bytes of the frame is received. Which interface counter increments?

A. runt.

B. collision.

C. late collision.

D. CRC.

35)

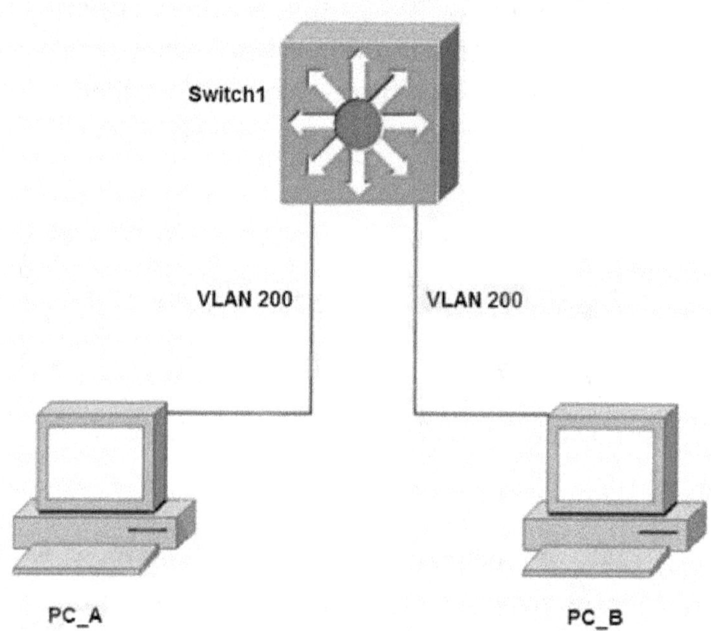

Refer to the exhibit. Which outcome is expected when PC_A sends data to PC_B?

A. The source MAC address is changed.

B. The destination MAC address is replaced with ffff.ffff.ffff.

C. The source and destination MAC addresses remain the same.

D. The switch rewrites the source and destination MAC addresses with its own.

36) Using direct sequence spread spectrum, which three 2.4-GHz channels are used to limit collisions?

A. 5, 6, 7

B. 1, 2, 3

C. 1, 6, 11

D. 1, 5, 10

37) How do TCP and UDP differ in the way they guarantee packet delivery?

A. TCP uses retransmissions, acknowledgment, and parity checks, and UDP uses cyclic redundancy checks only.

B. TCP uses two-dimensional parity checks, checksums, and cyclic redundancy checks, and UDP uses retransmissions only.

C. TCP uses checksum, acknowledgements, and retransmissions, and UDP uses checksums only.

D. TCP uses checksum, parity checks, and retransmissions, and UDP uses acknowledgements only.

38) A wireless administrator has configured a WLAN; however, the clients need access to a less congested 5-GHz network for their voice quality.

Which action must be taken to meet the requirement?

A. enable Band Select.

B. enable DTIM

C. enable RX-SOP.

D. enable AAA override.

39) What is the destination MAC address of a broadcast frame?

A. 00:00:0c:07:ac:01

B. ff:ff:ff:ff:ff:ff

C. 43:2e:08:00:00:0c

D. 00:00:0c:43:2e:08

E. 00:00:0c:ff:ff:ff

40) For what two purposes does the Ethernet protocol use physical addresses?

A. to uniquely identify devices at Layer 2.

B. to allow communication with devices on a different network.

C. to differentiate a Layer 2 frame from a Layer 3 packet.

D. to establish a priority system to determine which device gets to transmit first.

E. to allow communication between different devices on the same network.

F. to allow detection of a remote device when its physical address is unknown.

41) Which component of an Ethernet frame is used to notify a host that traffic is coming?

A. start of frame delimiter.

B. Type field.

C. preamble.

D. Data field.

42) You are configuring your edge routers interface with a public IP address for Internet connectivity. The router needs to obtain the IP address from the service provider dynamically.

Which command is needed on interface FastEthernet 0/0 to accomplish this?

A. ip default-gateway.

B. ip route.

C. ip default-network.

D. ip address dhcp.

E. ip address dynamic.

43) Which two statements about the purpose of the OSI model are accurate? (Choose two.)

A. Defines the network functions that occur at each layer.

B. Facilitates an understanding of how information travels throughout a network.

C. Changes in one layer do not impact another layer.

D. Ensures reliable data delivery through its layered approach.

44) Which three statements about MAC addresses are correct? (Choose three.)

A. To communicate with other devices on a network, a network device must have a unique MAC address.

B. The MAC address is also referred to as the IP address.

C. The MAC address of a device must be configured in the Cisco IOS CLI by a user with administrative privileges.

D. A MAC address contains two main components, the first of which identifies the manufacturer of the hardware and the second of which uniquely identifies the hardware.

E. An example of a MAC address is 0A:26:B8:D6:65:90.

F. A MAC address contains two main components, the first of which identifies the network on which the host resides and the second of which uniquely identifies the host on the network.

45) Which technique can you use to route IPv6 traffic over an IPv4 infrastructure?

A. NAT.

B. 6 to 4 tunneling.

C. L2TPv3.

D. dual-stack.

46) Refer to the exhibit. A network technician is asked to design a small network with redundancy.

The exhibit represents this design, with all hosts configured in the same VLAN.

What conclusions can be made about this design?

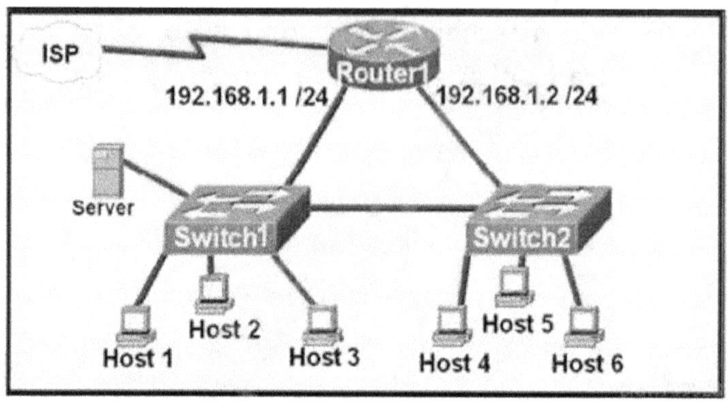

A. This design will function as intended.

B. Spanning-tree will need to be used.

C. The router will not accept the addressing scheme.

D. The connection between switches should be a trunk.

E. The router interfaces must be encapsulated with the 802.1Q protocol.

47) Which two statements are true about the command ip route 172.16.3.0 255.255.255.0 192.168.2.4? (Choose two.)

A. It establishes a static route to the 172.16.3.0 network.

B. It establishes a static route to the 192.168.2.0 network.

C. It configures the router to send any traffic for an unknown destination to the 172.16.3.0 network.

D. It configures the router to send any traffic for an unknown destination out the interface with the address 192.168.2.4.

E. It uses the default administrative distance.

F. It is a route that would be used last if other routes to the same destination exist.

48) What are two benefits of private IPv4 IP addresses? (Choose two.)

A. They are routed the same as public IP addresses.

B. They are less costly than public IP addresses.

C. They can be assigned to devices without Internet connections.

D. They eliminate the necessity for NAT policies.

E. They eliminate duplicate IP conflicts.

49) What are two benefits that the UDP protocol provide for application traffic? (Choose two.)

A. UDP traffic has lower overhead than TCP traffic.

B. UDP provides a built-in recovery mechanism to retransmit lost packets.

C. The CTL field in the UDP packet header enables a three-way handshake to establish the connection.

D. UDP maintains the connection state to provide more stable connections than TCP.

E. The application can use checksums to verify the integrity of application data.

50) Which two goals reasons to implement private IPv4 addressing on your network? (Choose two.)

A. Comply with PCI regulations.

B. Conserve IPv4 address.

C. Reduce the size of the forwarding table on network routers.

D. Reduce the risk of a network security breach.

E. Comply with local law.

51) Which WAN access technology is preferred for a small office / home office architecture?

A. broadband cable access.

B. frame-relay packet switching.

C. dedicated point-to-point leased line.

D. Integrated Services Digital Network switching.

52) Which two WAN architecture options help a business scalability and reliability for the network? (Choose two.)

A. asynchronous routing.

B. single-homed branches.

C. dual-homed branches.

D. static routing.

E. dynamic routing.

53) What is the binary pattern of unique ipv6 unique local address?

A. 00000000

B. 11111100

C. 11111111

D. 11111101

54) Which two options are the best reasons to use an IPV4 private IP space? (Choose two.)

A.   to   enable   intra-enterprise communication.

B. to implement NAT.

C. to connect applications.

D. to conserve global address space.

E. to manage routing overhead.

55) Refer to the exhibit. When PC1 sends a packet to PC2, the packet has which source and destination IP address when it arrives at interface Gi0/0 on router R2?

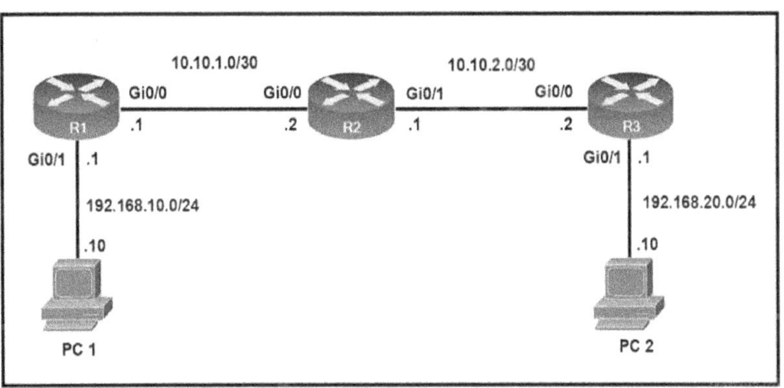

A. source 192.168.10.10 and destination 10.10.2.2

B. source 192.168.20.10 and destination 192.168.20.1

C. source 192.168.10.10 and destination 192.168.20.10

D. source 10.10.1.1 and destination 10.10.2.2

56) What is the same for both copper and fiber interfaces when using SFP modules?

A. They support an inline optical attenuator to enhance signal strength.

B. They accommodate single-mode and multi-mode in a single module.

C. They provide minimal interruption to services by being hot-swappable.

D. They offer reliable bandwidth up to 100 Mbps in half duplex mode.

57) What are two functions of a server on a network? (Choose two.)

A. handles requests from multiple workstations at the same time.

B. achieves redundancy by exclusively using virtual server clustering.

C. housed solely in a data center that is dedicated to a single client.

D. runs the same operating system in order to communicate with other servers.

E. runs applications that send and retrieve data for workstations that make requests.

58) Which function is performed by the collapsed core layer in a two-tier architecture?

A. enforcing routing policies.

B. marking interesting traffic for data policies.

C. applying security policies.

D. attaching users to the edge of the network.

59) What is the primary function of a Layer 3 device?

A. to transmit wireless traffic between hosts.

B. to analyze traffic and drop unauthorized traffic from the Internet.

C. to forward traffic within the same broadcast domain.

D. to pass traffic between different networks.

60) Which two functions are performed by the core layer in a three-tier architecture? (Choose two.)

A. Provide uninterrupted forwarding service.

B. Inspect packets for malicious activity.

C. Ensure timely data transfer between layers.

D. Provide direct connectivity for end user devices.

E. Police traffic that is sent to the edge of the network.

61) What is a recommended approach to avoid co-channel congestion while installing access points that use the 2.4 GHz frequency?

A. different nonoverlapping channels.

B. one overlapping channel.

C. one nonoverlapping channel.

D. different overlapping channels.

62) A manager asks a network engineer to advise which cloud service models are used so employees do not have to waste their time installing, managing, and updating software that is only used occasionally.

Which cloud service model does the engineer recommend?

A. infrastructure-as-a-service.

B. platform-as-a-service.

C. business process as service to support different types of service.

D. software-as-a-service.

63) What are two functions of a Layer 2 switch? (Choose two.)

A. acts as a central point for association and authentication servers.

B. selects the best route between networks on a WAN.

C. moves packets within a VLAN.

D. moves packets between different VLANs.

E. makes forwarding decisions based on the MAC address of a packet.

64) An engineer observes high usage on the 2.4GHz channels and lower usage on the 5GHz channels. What must be configured to allow clients to preferentially use 5GHz access points?

A. Client Band Select.

B. Re-Anchor Roamed Clients.

C. OEAP Spilt Tunnel.

D. 11ac MU-MIMO.

65) Which networking function occurs on the data plane?

A. processing inbound SSH management traffic.

B. sending and receiving OSPF Hello packets.

C. facilitates spanning-tree elections.

D. forwarding remote client/server traffic.

66) Under which condition is TCP preferred over UDP?

A. UDP is used when low latency is optimal, and TCP is used when latency is tolerable.

B. TCP is used when dropped data is more acceptable, and UDP is used when data is accepted out-of-order.

C. TCP is used when data reliability is critical, and UDP is used when missing packets are acceptable.

D. UDP is used when data is highly interactive, and TCP is used when data is time-sensitive.

67)

```
SiteA#show interface TenGigabitEthernet0/1/0
TenGigabitEthernet0/1/0 is up, line protocol is up
  Hardware is BUILT-IN-EPA-8x10G, address is 780c.f02a.db91 (bia 780a.f02b.db91)
  Description: Connection to SiteB
  Internet address is 10.10.10.1/30
  MTU 8146 bytes, BW 10000000 Kbit/sec, DLY 10 usec,
     reliability 166/255, txload 1/255, rxload 1/255
  Full Duplex, 10000Mbps, link type is force-up, media type is SFP-LR
  5 minute input rate 264797000 bits/sec, 26672 packets/sec
  5 minute output rate 122464000 bits/sec, 15724 packets/sec

SiteB#show interface TenGigabitEthernet0/1/0
TenGigabitEthernet0/1/0 is up, line protocol is up
  Hardware is BUILT-IN-EPA-8x10G, address is 780c.f02c.db26 (bia 780c.f02c.db26)
  Description: Connection to SiteA
  Internet address is 10.10.10.2/30
  MTU 8146 bytes, BW 10000000 Kbit/sec, DLY 10 usec,
     reliability 255/255, txload 1/255, rxload 1/255
  Full Duplex, 10000Mbps, link type is force-up, media type is SFP-LR
  5 minute input rate 122464000 bits/sec, 15724 packets/sec
  5 minute output rate 264797000 bits/sec, 26672 packets/sec
```

Refer to the exhibit. Shortly after SiteA was connected to SiteB over a new single-mode fiber path, users at SiteA report intermittent connectivity issues with applications hosted at SiteB.

What is the cause of the intermittent connectivity issue?

A. Interface errors are incrementing.

B. High usage is causing high latency.

C. An incorrect SFP media type was used at SiteA.

D. The sites were connected with the wrong cable type.

68) A network engineer must configure the router R1 GigabitEthernet1/1 interface to connect to the router R2 GigabitEthernet1/1 interface. For the configuration to be applied, the engineer must compress the address 2001:0db8:0000:0000:0500:000a:400F:58B.

Which command must be issued on the interface?

A. ipv6 address 2001::db8:0000::500:a:400F:583B

B. ipv6 address 2001:db8:0::500:a:4F:583B

C. ipv6 address 2001:db8::500:a:400F:583B

D. ipv6 address 2001:0db8::5:a:4F:583B

69) What is a network appliance that checks the state of a packet to determine whether the packet is legitimate?

A. Layer 2 switch.

B. LAN controller.

C. load balancer.

D. firewall.

70) What is a role of access points in an enterprise network?

A. integrate with SNMP in preventing DDoS attacks.

B. serve as a first line of defense in an enterprise network.

C. connect wireless devices to a wired network.

D. support secure user logins to devices on the network.

71) An implementer is preparing hardware for virtualization to create virtual machines on a host. What is needed to provide communication between hardware and virtual machines?

A. router.

B. hypervisor.

C. switch.

D. straight cable.

72) How does a Cisco Unified Wireless Network respond to Wi-Fi channel overlap?

A. It allows the administrator to assign the channels on a per-device or per-interface basis.

B. It segregates devices from different manufactures onto different channels.

C. It analyzes client load and background noise and dynamically assigns a channel.

D. It alternates automatically between 2.4 GHz and 5 GHz on adjacent access points.

73) In which situation is private IPv4 addressing appropriate for a new subnet on the network of an organization?

A. The network has multiple endpoint listeners, and it is desired to limit the number of broadcasts.

B. The ISP requires the new subnet to be advertised to the Internet for web services.

C. There is limited unique address space, and traffic on the new subnet will stay local within the organization.

D. Traffic on the subnet must traverse a site-to-site VPN to an outside organization.

74) Which 802.11 frame type is indicated by a probe response after a client sends a probe request?

A. data.

B. management.

C. control.

D. action.

75) What is the difference in data transmission delivery and reliability between TCP and UDP?

A. TCP transmits data at a higher rate and ensures packet delivery. UDP retransmits lost data to ensure applications receive the data on the remote end.

B. TCP requires the connection to be established before transmitting data. UDP transmits data at a higher rate without ensuring packet delivery.

C. UDP sets up a connection between both devices before transmitting data. TCP uses the three-way handshake to transmit data with a reliable connection.

D. UDP is used for multicast and broadcast communication. TCP is used for unicast communication and transmits data at a higher rate with error checking.

76)

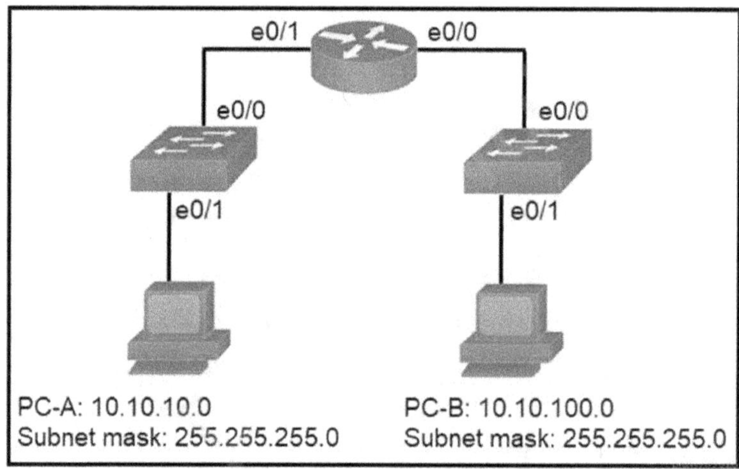

Refer to the exhibit. When PC-A sends traffic to PC-B, which network component is in charge of receiving the packet from PC-A, verifying the IP addresses, and forwarding the packet to PC-B?

A. router.

B. Layer 2 switch.

C. load balancer.

D. firewall.

77) What is the maximum bandwidth of a T1 point-to-point connection?

A. 1.544 Mbps.

B. 2.048 Mbps.

C. 34.368 Mbps.

D. 43.7 Mbps.

78) What are two similarities between UTP Cat 5e and Cat 6a cabling? (Choose two.)

A. Both support speeds up to 10 Gigabit.

B. Both support speeds of at least 1 Gigabit.

C. Both support runs of up to 55 meters.

D. Both support runs of up to 100 meters.

E. Both operate at a frequency of 500 MHz.

79) What is a characteristic of cloud-based network topology?

A. onsite network services are provided with physical Layer 2 and Layer 3 components.

B. wireless connections provide the sole access method to services.

C. physical workstations are configured to share resources.

D. services are provided by a public, private, or hybrid deployment.

80) Which network action occurs within the data plane?

A. reply to an incoming ICMP echo request.

B. make a configuration change from an incoming NETCONF RPC.

C. run routing protocols (OSPF, EIGRP, RIP, BGP).

D. compare the destination IP address to the IP routing table.

81)

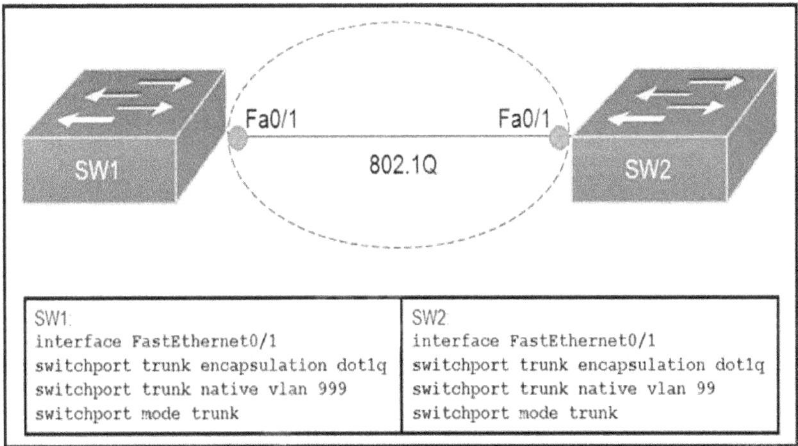

SW1:	SW2:
interface FastEthernet0/1	interface FastEthernet0/1
switchport trunk encapsulation dot1q	switchport trunk encapsulation dot1q
switchport trunk native vlan 999	switchport trunk native vlan 99
switchport mode trunk	switchport mode trunk

Refer to the exhibit. Which action do the switches take on the trunk link?

A. The trunk does not form, and the ports go into an err-disabled status.

B. The trunk forms, but the mismatched native VLANs are merged into a single broadcast domain.

C. The trunk forms, but VLAN 99 and VLAN 999 are in a shutdown state.

D. The trunk does not form, but VLAN 99 and VLAN 999 are allowed to traverse the link.

82) What is the primary effect of the spanning-tree port fast command?

A. It immediately enables the port in the listening state.

B. It immediately puts the port into the forwarding state when the switch is reloaded.

C. It enables BPDU messages.

D. It minimizes spanning-tree convergence time.

83) What occurs when Port Fast is enabled on an interface that is connected to another switch?

A. Root port choice and spanning-tree recalculation are accelerated when a switch link goes down.

B. After spanning-tree converges, Port Fast shuts down any port that receives BPDUs.

C. VTP is allowed to propagate VLAN configuration information from switch to switch automatically.

D. Spanning-tree fails to detect a switching loop increasing the likelihood of broadcast storms.

84) Which QoS Profile is selected in the GUI when configuring a voice over WLAN deployment?

A. Platinum.

B. Bronze.

C. Gold.

D. Silver.

85)

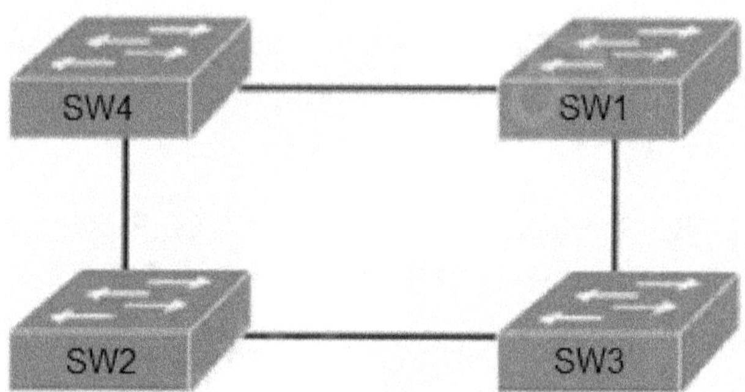

Refer to the exhibit. Which switch in this configuration will be elected as the root bridge?

SW1: 0C:E0:38:41:86:07 -

SW2: 0C:0E:15:22:05:97 -

SW3: 0C:0E:15:1A:3C:9D -

SW4: 0C:E0:18:A1:B3:19 -

A. SW1

B. SW2

C. SW3

D. SW4

86) An engineer needs to configure LLDP to send the port description type length value (TLV). Which command sequence must be implemented?

A. switch(config-if)#lldp port-description.

B. switch#lldp port-description.

C. switch(config-line)#lldp port-description.

D. switch(config)#lldp port-description.

87)

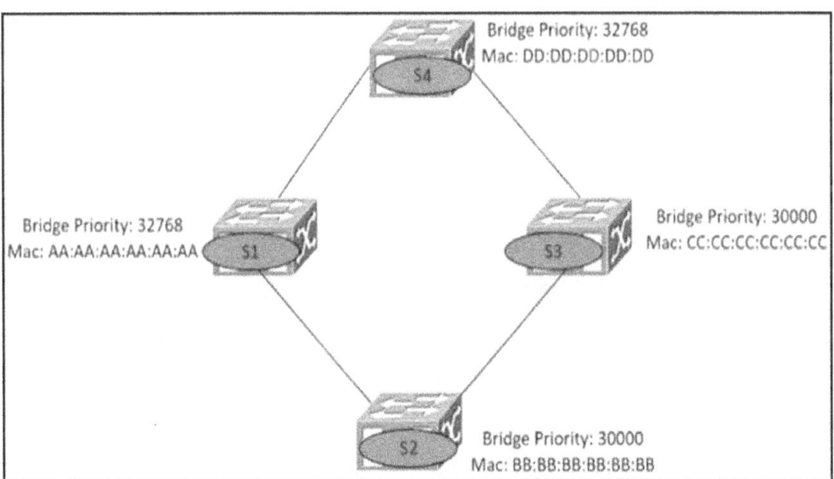

Refer to the exhibit. Which switch becomes the root bridge?

A. S1

B. S2

C. S3

D. S4

88) Which configuration ensures that the switch is always the root for VLAN 750?

A. Switch(config)#spanning-tree vlan 750 priority 38418607

B. Switch(config)#spanning-tree vlan 750 priority 0

C. Switch(config)#spanning-tree vlan 750 root primary

D. Switch(config)#spanning-tree vlan 750 priority 614440

89)

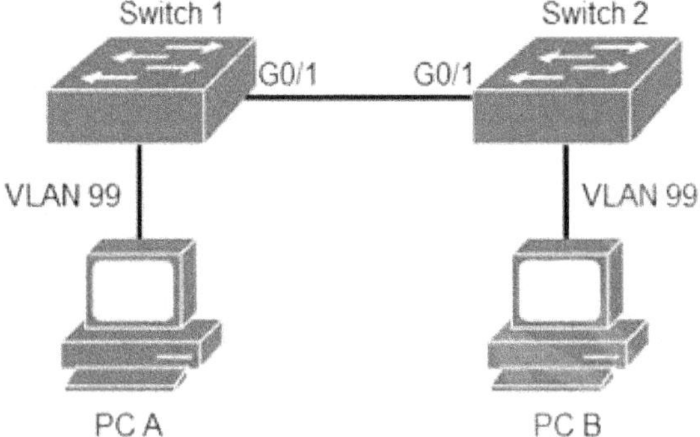

Switch 1:
```
Name: Gi0/1
Switchport: Enabled
Administrative Mode: trunk
Operational Mode: trunk
Administrative Trunking Encapsulation: dot1q
Operational Trunking Encapsulation: dot1q
Negotiation of Trunking: Off
Access Mode VLAN: 1 (default)
Trunking Native Mode VLAN: 1 (default)
Administrative Native VLAN tagging: enabled
Voice VLAN: none
[output omitted]
Trunking VLANs Enabled: 50-100
Pruning VLANs Enabled: 2-1001
Capture Mode Disabled
Capture VLANs Allowed: ALL
```

```
Switch 2:
Name: Gi0/1
Switchport: Enabled
Administrative Mode: trunk
Operational Mode: trunk
Administrative Trunking Encapsulation: dot1q
Operational Trunking Encapsulation: dot1q
Negotiation of Trunking: Off
Access Mode VLAN: 1 (default)
Trunking Native Mode VLAN: 99 (VLAN0099)
Administrative Native VLAN tagging: enabled
Voice VLAN: none
[output omitted]
Trunking VLANs Enabled: 50-100
Pruning VLANs Enabled: 2-1001
Capture Mode Disabled
Capture VLANs Allowed: ALL
```

Refer to the exhibit. After the switch configuration, the ping test fails between PC A and PC B. Based on the output for switch 1, which error must be corrected?

A. The PCs are in the incorrect VLAN.

B. All VLANs are not enabled on the trunk.

C. Access mode is configured on the switch ports.

D. There is a native VLAN mismatch.

90) Which unified access point mode continues to serve wireless clients after losing connectivity to the Cisco Wireless LAN Controller?

A. local.

B. mesh.

C. flexconnect.

D. sniffer.

91)

```
Router#
Capability Codes: R - Router, T - Trans Bridge, B - Source Route Bridge
            S -Switch, H - Host, I - IGMP, r - Repeater, P - Phone,
            D - Remote, C - CVTA, M - Two-port Mac Relay

Device ID    Local Interface Holdtime Capability    Platform    Port ID
10.1.1.2     Gig 37/3        176             R I     CPT 600     Gig 36/41
10.1.1.2     Gig 37/1        174             R I     CPT 600     Gig 36/43
10.1.1.2     Gig 36/41       134             R I     CPT 600     Gig 37/3
10.1.1.2     Gig 36/43       134             R I     CPT 600     Gig 37/1
10.1.1.2     Ten 3/2         132             R I     CPT 600     Ten 4/2
10.1.1.2     Ten 4/2         174             R I     CPT 600     Ten 3/2
```

Refer to the exhibit. Which command provides this output?

A. show IP route.

B. show CDP neighbor.

C. show IP interface.

D. show interface.

92) Which mode must be used to configure EtherChannel between two switches without using a negotiation protocol?

A. active.

B. on.

C. auto.

D. desirable.

93) Which mode allows access points to be managed by Cisco Wireless LAN Controllers?

A. bridge.

B. lightweight.

C. mobility express.

D. autonomous.

94) Which two values or settings must be entered when configuring a new WLAN in the Cisco Wireless LAN Controller GUI? (Choose two.)

A. QoS settings.

B. IP address of one or more access points.

C. SSID.

D. profile name.

E. management interface settings.

95) Which command is used to specify the delay time in seconds for LLDP to initialize on any interface?

A. lldp timer.

B. lldp tlv-select.

C. lldp reinit.

D. lldp holdtime.

96)

```
SW2
vtp domain cisco
vtp mode transparent
vtp password ciscotest
interface fastethernet0/1
    description connection to sw1
    switchport mode trunk
    switchport trunk encapsulation dot1q
```

Refer to the exhibit. How does SW2 interact with other switches in this VTP domain?

A. It transmits and processes VTP updates from any VTP clients on the network on its trunk ports.

B. It processes VTP updates from any VTP clients on the network on its access ports.

C. It receives updates from all VTP servers and forwards all locally configured VLANs out all trunk ports.

D. It forwards only the VTP advertisements that it receives on its trunk ports.

97)

```
SW1#sh lacp neighbor
Flags:  S - Device is requesting Slow LACPDUs
        F - Device is requesting Fast LACPDUs
        A - Device is in Active mode      P - Device is in Passive mode

Channel group 35 neighbors

Partner's information:

                LACP port                       Admin Oper  Port    Port
Port    Flags  Priority    Dev ID          Age  key   Key   Number  State
Et1/0   SP     32768       aabb.cc80.7000  8s   0x0   0x23  0x101   0x3C
Et1/1   SP     32768       aabb.cc80.7000  8s   0x0   0x23  0x102   0x3C
```

Refer to the exhibit. Based on the LACP neighbor status, in which mode is the SW1 port channel configured?

A. mode on.

B. active.

C. passive.

D. auto.

98) Two switches are connected and using Cisco Dynamic Trunking Protocol. SW1 is set to Dynamic Auto and SW2 is set to Dynamic Desirable. What is the result of this configuration?

A. The link becomes an access port.

B. The link is in an error disabled state.

C. The link is in a down state.

D. The link becomes a trunk port.

99) A Cisco IP phone receives untagged data traffic from an attached PC. Which action is taken by the phone?

A. It drops the traffic.

B. It allows the traffic to pass through unchanged.

C. It tags the traffic with the native VLAN.

D. It tags the traffic with the default VLAN.

100) Which design element is a best practice when deploying an 802.11b wireless infrastructure?

A. allocating nonoverlapping channels to access points that are in close physical proximity to one another.

B. disabling TCP so that access points can negotiate signal levels with their attached wireless devices.

C. configuring access points to provide clients with a maximum of 5 Mbps.

D. setting the maximum data rate to 54 Mbps on the Cisco Wireless LAN Controller.

101) Refer to the exhibit. The network administrator wants VLAN 67 traffic to be untagged between Switch 1 and Switch 2, while all other VLANs are to remain tagged.

Which command accomplishes this task?

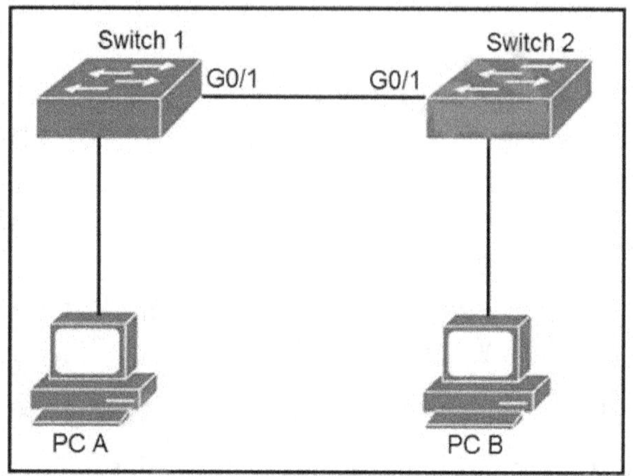

A. switchport access vlan 67

B. switchport trunk allowed vlan 67

C. switchport private-vlan association host 67

D. switchport trunk native vlan 67

102) Which two command sequences must be configured on a switch to establish a Layer 3 EtherChannel with an open-standard protocol?

(Choose two.)

A. interface GigabitEthernet0/0/1 channel-group 10 mode auto

B. interface GigabitEthernet0/0/1 channel-group 10 mode on..

C. interface port-channel 10 no switchport ip address 172.16.0.1 255.255.255.0

D. interface GigabitEthernet0/0/1 channel-group 10 mode active.

E. interface port-channel 10 switchport switchport mode trunk.

103) Refer to the exhibit. Which two commands when used together create port channel 10? (Choose two.)

```
Switch#show etherchannel summary
 [output omitted]

Group      Port-channel      Protocol      Ports
-------------+---------------------+----------------------+----------------------------------------
10            Po10(SU)          LACP          Gi0/0(P)      Gi0/1(P)
20            Po20(SU)          LACP          Gi0/2(P)      Gi0/3(P)
```

A. int range g0/0-1 channel-group 10 mode active.

B. int range g0/0-1 channel-group 10 mode desirable.

C. int range g0/0-1 channel-group 10 mode passive.

D. int range g0/0-1 channel-group 10 mode auto.

E. int range g0/0-1 channel-group 10 mode on.

104) Refer to the exhibit. An administrator is tasked with configuring a voice VLAN.

What is the expected outcome when a Cisco phone is connected to the GigabitEthernet 3/1/4 port on a switch?

```
interface GigabitEthernet3/1/4
  switchport voice vlan 50
!
```

A. The phone and a workstation that is connected to the phone do not have VLAN connectivity.

B. The phone sends and receives data in VLAN 50, but a workstation connected to the phone sends and receives data in VLAN 1.

C. The phone sends and receives data in VLAN 50, but a workstation connected to the phone has no VLAN connectivity.

D. The phone and a workstation that is connected to the phone send and receive data in VLAN 50.

105) Refer to the exhibit. Which action is expected from SW1 when the untagged frame is received on the GigabitEthernet0/1 interface?

```
SW1#show run int gig 0/1
interface GigabitEthernet0/1
  switchport access vlan 11
  switchport trunk allowed vlan 1-10
  switchport trunk encapsulation dot1q
  switchport trunk native vlan 5
  switchport mode trunk
  speed 1000
  duplex full
```

A. The frame is processed in VLAN 1

B. The frame is processed in VLAN 11

C. The frame is processed in VLAN 5

D. The frame is dropped

106) Which command is used to enable LLDP globally on a Cisco IOS ISR?

A. lldp run.

B. lldp enable.

C. lldp transmit.

D. cdp run.

E. cdp enable.

107) Which command should you enter to configure an LLDP delay time of 5 seconds?

A. lldp timer 5000

B. lldp holdtime 5

C. lldp reinit 5000

D. lldp reinit 5

108) In a CDP environment, what happens when the CDP interface on an adjacent device is configured without an IP address?

A. CDP becomes inoperable on that neighbor.

B. CDP uses the IP address of another interface for that neighbor.

C. CDP operates normally, but it cannot provide IP address information for that neighbor.

D. CDP operates normally, but it cannot provide any information for that neighbor.

109) When configuring an EtherChannel bundle, which mode enables LACP only if a LACP device is detected?

A. Passive.

B. Desirable.

C. On.

D. Auto.

E. Active.

110) Refer to the exhibit. Which VLAN ID is associated with the default VLAN in the given environment?

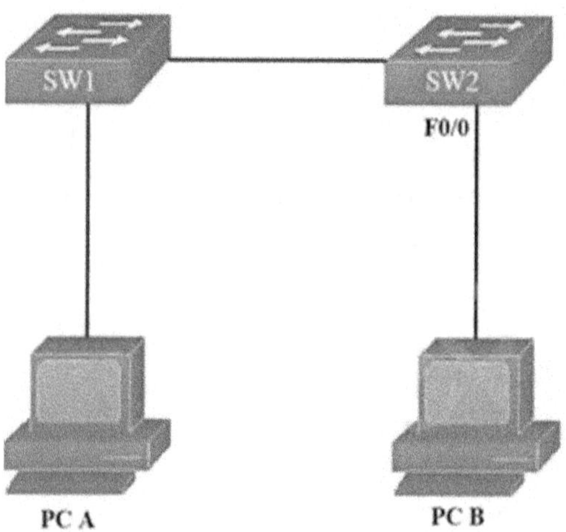

```
SW1
interface FastEthernet0/0
    switchport mode access
    switchport access vlan 5
interface FastEthernet0/1
    switchport mode trunk
    switchport trunk allow vlan 5-20
    switchport trunk native vlan 10


SW2
interface FastEthernet0/0
    switchport mode access
    switchport access vlan 5
interface FastEthernet0/1
    switchport mode trunk
    switchport trunk allow vlan 5-20
    switchport trunk native vlan 10
```

A. VLAN 1

B. VLAN 5

C. VLAN 10

D. VLAN 20

111) Which two VLAN IDs indicate a default VLAN?

(Choose two.)

A. 0

B. 1

C. 1005

D. 1006

E. 4096

112) Which two pieces of information about a Cisco device can Cisco Discovery Protocol communicate?

(Choose two.)

A. the native VLAN.

B. the trunking protocol.

C. the VTP domain.

D. the spanning-tree priority.

E. the spanning-tree protocol.

113) After you deploy a new WLAN controller on your network, which two

additional tasks should you consider? (Choose two.)

A. deploy load balancers.

B. configure additional vlans.

C. configure multiple VRRP groups.

D. deploy POE switches.

E. configure additional security policies.

114) Refer to the exhibit. How will switch SW2 handle traffic from VLAN 10 on SW1?

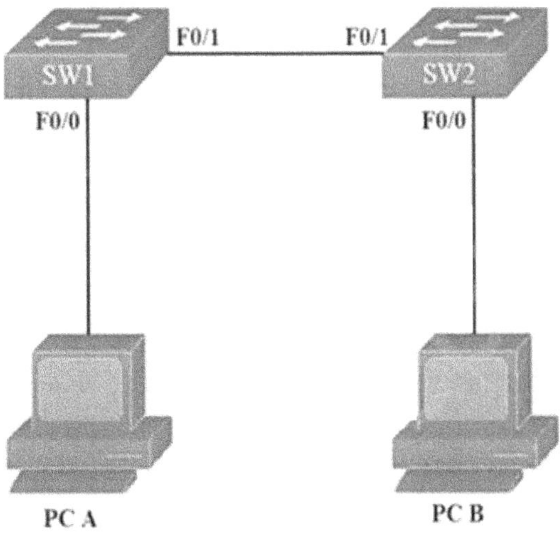

```
SW1
interface FastEthernet0/0
    switchport mode access
    switchport access vlan 5
interface FastEthernet0/1
    switchport mode trunk
    switchport trunk allow vlan 5-20
    switchport trunk native vlan 10


SW2
interface FastEthernet0/0
    switchport mode access
    switchport access vlan 5
interface FastEthernet0/1
    switchport mode trunk
    switchport trunk allow vlan 5-20
    switchport trunk native vlan 100
```

A. It sends the traffic to VLAN 10.

B. It sends the traffic to VLAN 100.

C. It drops the traffic.

D. It sends the traffic to VLAN 1.

115) Which two commands can you use to configure an actively negotiate EtherChannel? (Choose two.)

A. channel-group 10 mode on.

B. channel-group 10 mode auto.

C. channel-group 10 mode passive.

D. channel-group 10 mode desirable.

E. channel-group 10 mode active.

116) How does STP prevent forwarding loops at OSI Layer 2?

A. TTL.

B. MAC address forwarding.

C. Collision avoidance.

D. Port blocking.

117) Which two statements about VTP are true? (Choose two.)

A. All switches must be configured with the same VTP domain name.

B. All switches must be configured to perform trunk negotiation.

C. All switches must be configured with a unique VTP domain name.

D. The VTP server must have the highest revision number in the domain.

E. All switches must use the same VTP version.

118) Which type does a port become when it receives the best BPDU on a bridge?

A. The designated port.

B. The backup port.

C. The alternate port.

D. The root port.

119) Which value can you modify to configure a specific interface as the preferred forwarding interface?

A. The interface number.

B. The port priority.

C. The VLAN priority.

D. The hello time.

120) Which statement about Cisco Discovery Protocol is true?

A. It is a Cisco-proprietary protocol.

B. It runs on the network layer.

C. It can discover information from routers, firewalls, and switches.

D. It runs on the physical layer and the data link layer.

Answers & Explanation:

1) B

the route is learned within a network route 10.10.13.10/25, if it was 10.10.13.10/32 in that table it was a host route, if it was 0.0.0.0/0 it was a default route and so on.

*Network route represent Network

*Router always prefers most specific route in routing table so this means router selects the longest prefix (Most specific) Routing.

2) D

10.10.13.208/29 gives .208 for network, hmin 209, hmax 214, bcast 215.

The prefix with "longest prefix" will be matched first.

3) Correct Answer: AD

Whenever the physical transmission has problems, the receiving device might receive a frame whose bits have changed values. These frames do not pass the error detection logic as implemented in the FCS field in the Ethernet trailer. The receiving device discards the frame and counts it as some kind of input error.

Cisco switches list this error as a CRC error. Cyclic redundancy check (CRC) is a term related to how the FCS math detects an error.

The "input errors" includes runts, giants, no buffer, CRC, frame, overrun, and ignored counts.

The output below shows the interface counters with the "show interface s0/0/0" command:

```
Router#show interface s0/0/0
Serial0/0/0 is up, line protocol is up
  Hardware is M4T
  Description: Link to R2
  Internet address is 10.1.1.1/30
  MTU 1500 bytes, BW 1544 Kbit, DLY 20000 usec,
     reliability 255/255, txload 1/255, rxload 1/255
  --output omitted--
  5 minute output rate 0 bits/sec, 0 packets/sec
     268 packets input, 24889 bytes, 0 no buffer
     Received 0 broadcasts, 0 runts, 0 giants, 0 throttles
     0 input errors, 0 CRC, 0 frame, 0 overrun, 0 ignored, 0 abort
     251 packets output, 23498 bytes, 0 underruns
     0 output errors, 0 collisions, 0 interface resets
     0 output buffer failures, 0 output buffers swapped out
     0 carrier transitions    DCD=up  DSR=up  DTR=up  RTS=up  CTS=up
```

4) A

Reference:

https://www.guru99.com/tcp-vs-udp-understanding-the-difference.html#:~:text=TCP%20is%20a%20connection%2Doriented,UDP%20uses%20no%20handshake%20protocols&text=TCP%20has%20acknowledgment%20segments%2C%20but,not%20have%20any%20acknowledgment%20segment.

5) A

There are three main types of 802.11 frames: the Data Frame, the Management Frame and the Control Frame. Association Response belongs to Management Frame. Association response is sent in response to an association request.

Video on the 3 types of 802.11 frames:

https://www.youtube.com/watch?v=PCpnRqKCWCQ

6) C

In Spine Leaf architecture...

To increase performance(bandwidth) - Add Spine switch connects to every Leaf Switch.

To Increase Access switch ports count - Add leaf switch and connects to every Spine switch.

Spine-leaf architecture is typically deployed as two layers: spines (such as an aggregation layer), and leaves (such as an access layer). Spine-leaf topologies provide high-bandwidth, low-latency, nonblocking server-to-server connectivity.

Leaf (aggregation) switches are what provide devices access to the fabric (the network of spine and leaf switches) and are typically deployed at the top of the rack. Generally, devices connect to the leaf switches. Devices can include servers, Layer 4-7 services (firewalls and load balancers), and WAN or Internet routers.

Leaf switches do not connect to other leaf switches. In spine-and-leaf architecture, every leaf should connect to every spine in a full mesh.

Spine (aggregation) switches are used to connect to all leaf switches and are typically deployed at the end or middle of the row. Spine switches do not connect to other spine switches.

Reference:

https://www.cisco.com/c/en/us/products/collateral/switches/nexus-7000-series-switches/white-paper-c11-737022.html

7) C

8) B

The needed is an IPv6 address generated from a specified prefix and not from a delegated one.

9) C

If the destination MAC address is not in the CAM table (unknown destination MAC address), the switch sends the frame out all other ports that are in the same VLAN as the received frame. This is called flooding. It does not flood the frame out the same port on which the frame was received.

Whenever a switch receives a frame, it look f MAC address table for a matching entry and if not found, switch will forward to

(Flood) all the ports in the switch except the port that received.

10) D

The up in A is a broadcast.

/30 means 2 host bits left over =2^2=4. subtract 2 to give us 2 usable host IP addresses, and based on the mask of a /30 = .252

11) B

Private Address Ranges

Class A 10.0.0.0 to 10.255.255.255

Class B 172.16.0.0 to 172.32.255.255

class C 192.168.0.0 to 192.168.255.255

So, 172.28.0.0/16 in the range of Private IPs in Class B.

12) D

Because the next subnet address is 192.168.16.144

13) B

A IPv6 Unique Local Address is an IPv6 address in the block FC00::/7. It is the approximate IPv6 counterpart of the IPv4 private address. It is not routable on the global Internet.

Note: In the past, Site-local addresses (FEC0::/10) are equivalent to private IP addresses in IPv4 but now they are deprecated.

Link-local addresses only used for communications within the local subnet. It is usually created dynamically using a link-local prefix of FE80::/10 and a 64-bit interface identifier (based on 48-bit MAC address).

14) D

IPV6

1.Unicast

2.Any Cast

3.Multicast(FF00::/8)

Uni-cast

----

i.Global Uni cast (Public IPs 2000::/3)

ii.Unique Local (Private IPs FD00::/8)

iii.Link Local (FE08::10)

group address means one to many (Multicast).

FF00::/8 is used for IPv6 multicast and this is the IPv6 type of address the question wants to ask.

FE80::/10 range is used for link-local addresses. Link-local addresses only used for communications within the local subnetwork (automatic address configuration, neighbor discovery, router discovery, and by many routing protocols). It is only valid on the current subnet. It is usually created dynamically using a link-local prefix of FE80::/10 and a 64-bit interface identifier (based on 48-bit MAC address).

15) BE

A late collision is defined as any collision that occurs after the first 512 bits (or 64th byte) of the frame have been transmitted. The usual possible causes are full-duplex/half-duplex mismatch, exceeded Ethernet cable length limits, or defective hardware such as incorrect cabling, non-compliant number of hubs in the network, or a bad NIC.

Late collisions should never occur in a properly designed Ethernet network. They usually occur when Ethernet cables are too long or when there are too many repeaters in the network.

When Carrier Sense Multiple Access/Collision Detection is used was the result f the collision domain but not the reason.

Reference:

https://www.cisco.com/en/US/docs/intern etworking/troubleshooting/guide/tr1904.ht ml

16) A

A wireless LAN (or WLAN) controller is used in combination with the Lightweight Access Point Protocol (LWAPP) to "manage lightweight access points in large quantities" by the network administrator or network operations center.

D could also be correct if there is no autonomous wording. Autonomous doesn't support LWAPP protocol (Autonomous Ap's are standalone Ap's which does not support CAPWAP/LWAPP) that Wireless Lan Controller uses).

17) A

PoE monitoring and policing compares the power consumption on ports with the administrative maximum value (either a configured maximum value or the port's default value). If the power consumption on a monitored port exceeds the administrative maximum value, the following actions occur:

- A syslog message is issued.

- The monitored port is shut down and error-disabled.

- The allocated power is freed.

Reference:

https://www.cisco.com/c/en/us/td/docs/switches/lan/catalyst6500/ios/12-2SX/configuration/guide/book/power_over_ethernet.pdf

18) C

Frame flooding would be restricted to the devices that are in that VLAN. With a potential loop issue the flooding could occur from the switch NOT having a device match nor location in the MAC table. B would describe a broadcast.

19) A

20) C

Reference:

https://howdoesinternetwork.com/2013/sl aac-ipv6-stateless-address-autoconfiguration

21) CE

C and E have somehow the same meaning: avoid signal overlapping, since E separate the channel to avoid using the same channel and having signal collision. See "Dynamic Channel Assignment" in https://www.cisco.com/c/en/us/td/docs/wi

reless/controller/8-5/config-guide/b_cg85/radio_resource_managemen t.html

A and B are kind of tricky to mention 5GHz, which must have non-overlapping channels, and actually accomplish what C/E have done, but they're saying incorrect stuff.

For A: 2.4GHz has 11 Channels, 5GHZ has 45 Channels

For B: There are two types of APs: autonomous AP/controllerless AP/"Fat AP" and lightweight AP/AP with Controller.

And lightweight AP can be applied to 2.4GHz and 5Hz (there's command for both in cisco lightweight AP, just google it....

For D: the repeater cannot solve the problem of "overlapping channels" since it just re-transmits or "repeat" the signal, aka the overlapping channels will still be overlapping.

Reference:

https://stormwindstudios.com/wireless-access-points/

22) B

23) BD

1.There are 3 kind of wiring mainly when we talk about networking: Fiber, Coaxial cable, twisted pair. The last 2 are Copper wiring.

2. BNC Connector is for Coaxial Cable, so A is wrong.

3.the structure of fiber is: Jacket encase Buffer, Buffer encases Cladding, Cladding encase core. We use light to transmit data through the core. Therefore, B and D are right, C is wrong.

4. RJ45 is a connector is for twisted pair, so E is wrong.

24) D

A, B, and C all are connection related.

D is the only answer that relates to "communication".

25) D

FF <- easiest way to remember multicast.

26) D

27) AB

Core: Aggregates distribution switches in very large campus LANs, providing very high forwarding rates for the larger volume of traffic due to the size of the network.

Only switching between campus (distribution) switches should be performed at the core layer. Nothing should be done to slow down forwarding of traffic, such as using ACLs, supporting clients, or routing between VLANs.

Core layer switches are commonly set up in a star topology. This is because core layer switches connect multiple campuses via distribution layer switches.

28) D

Global unicast addresses (GUAs), also known as aggregable global unicast addresses, are globally routable and reachable in the IPv6 Internet. They are equivalent to public IPv4 addresses. They play a significant role in the IPv6 addressing architecture.

29) C

EUI-64 Process

01.Split Mac Address in to two (00:BB:CC | DD:11:22)

02. Insert FFFE Hexa in the middle

Eg: 00:BB:CC:DD:11:22 --> 02BB:CCFF:FEDD:1122

03.Invert the 7th Bit of the MAC address (0 to 1)

Reference:

https://geek-university.com/ccna/ipv6-eui-64-calculation/

30) C

network summary each floor,

max user to each floor=30<=2^H-2

H=5, will give N=3 therefore /27

For Network Summary,

Total Users, = 103

103<=2^H-2

H=7

will give N=1

Therefore/25

The main goal is always to make efficient use of IPs (Waste as little as possible). "B" &

"D" it is not enough to cover all the users for each floor.

31) D

Find the subnet mask

*To have 20 User in a subnet We have to use /27 prefix

* So Host count for /27 prefix is (2^5-2)=30

* Subnet Mask for /27 prefix is (sum of Network bits (128+64+32)=224 , so 255.255.255.224

Find the network ID

*As per the /27 prefix each subnet has 30 host and 32 including network ID & Broadcast ID

* So, first network ID is 10.10.255.0 and the second will be 10.10.255.32

32) D

There are no direct links between leaf switches, so D is correct.

33) B

40*8<=2^H-2, will give H=9 which is a /23 OR 255.255.254.0

34) C

Collision happens after 512 bits =64 byte =late collision.

35) C

The easy part here is that the data does not need to cross a router to reach a different network PC A sends a ping (or anything to PC B).

Switch doesn't yet know who is PC B and forwards that via broadcast to all ports in same VLAN minus the originating port.

PC B in same VLAN responds and now switch has both MAC addresses and their respective ports in CAM table.

MAC info in switch CAM does not change since both PC's are in same VLAN and do not need to cross a router (which WOULD change the destination and source MAC).

The MAC address does not change when a switch does not have the destination MAC in its CAM table. It DOES NOT become a broadcast packet; the switch just floods the traffic to all ports (minus the receiving port) and only the device with the correct MAC will process the packet (all other devices will drop the packet). If the MAC were changed to the broadcast MAC ALL devices would need to process the packet to determine the IP address.

36) C

Collisions happen in a wired network; congestion happens in a wireless network.

37) C

C. TCP uses checksum, acknowledgements, and retransmissions, and UDP uses checksums only.

38) A

Reference:

https://rscciew.wordpress.com/2014/10/26
/cisco-band-select-
feature/#:~:text=We%20can%20configure%
20this%20feature,applications%20(Like%3A
%20Voice)

39) B

Related question to this could be the
address' range used by HRSP:
0000.0C9F.F000 to 0000.0C9F.FFFF.

40) AE

(F) is incorrect, because remote device
means it belongs to another network.

41) C

Preamble is a 7 Byte field in the Ethernet
frame which helps to receiver to know that
it is an actual data (Ethernet Frame) and not

some random noise in the transmission medium. It acts like a doorbell talking about the incoming data.

42) D

means that the router will act as a DHCP client.

Should a router be set as a DHCP server commands are as follows:

conf t

service dhcp

ip dhcp pool <pool name>

network <network to be use as pool>

default-router <default gateway or the ip address of the ethernet interface facing the host>

dns-server <ip add of your dns server, say: 8.8.8.8 which is a google dns>exit.

43) AB

C is incorrect because changes in one layer definitely affects others; imagine affecting layer 1 (disconnect a cable, plug it incorrectly, administer the incorrect amount of voltage, etc), it would affect other layers.

D is incorrect because OSI model is not meant to ensure anything, it simply explains some of the features of each layer it defines.

44) ADE

45) B

Overlay tunneling encapsulates IPv6 packets in IPv4 packets for delivery across an IPv4 infrastructure (a core network or the figure below). By using overlay tunnels, you can communicate with isolated IPv6 networks without upgrading the IPv4 infrastructure between them. Overlay tunnels can be configured between border devices or between a border device and a host; however, both tunnel endpoints must support both the IPv4 and IPv6 protocol stacks. IPv6 supports the following types of overlays tunneling mechanisms:

1 Manual

2 Generic routing encapsulations (GRE)

3 IPv4-compatible

4 6to4

5 Intra-site Automatic Tunnel Addressing Protocol (ISATAP).

46) C

Each router interface Must be in different network.

Each interface on a router must be in a different network. If two interfaces are in the same network, the router will not accept it and show error when the administrator assigns it.

47) AE

The tricky part to the question is the prefix subnet 172.16.3.0 which is the destination network. B is wrong. The 192.168.2.0 network is the next hop used to reach the static route destination. No metric is set so the default value of 6 will be used for the administrative distance.

https://www.cisco.com/c/en/us/td/docs/routers/nfvis/switch_command/b-nfvis-switch-command-reference/ip_route_commands.pdf

48) BC

B is correct because they're free.

C is correct because local devices can still communicate with private IP's without internet.

D is not correct because a duplicate IP address can still be configured by accident via human error.

49) AE

50) BD

51) A

Broadband is correct for small office.

52) CE

Dynamic routing serves scalability as compared to static routing.

53) D

According to latest RFC, unique local address is FD00::/8

54) AD

55) C

The source and destination IP addresses of the packets are unchanged on all the way. Only source and destination MAC addresses are changed.

56) C

Hot-Swap-Component that of device can be removed or install without powering down the device.

57) AE

58) A

59) D

60) AC

Things like packet inspection is a separate network service and is not part of the 3-tier architecture model.

Also think about network design with network virtualization. The inspection of the workload traffic can be completely decoupled of the physical layers.

61) A

Each AP operates in one channel. The goal is that neighboring APs don't use the same channel, so you need multiple non-overlapping channels, or you have co-channel interference, which slows down your wireless operation. (Adjacent channel interference causes collisions).

62) D

SaaS provides the required Software, operating system and network:

Provides ready-to-use application or software.

63) CE

64) A

Band Select is Cisco's terminology for Band Steering. When enabled it encourages stations onto the 5 GHz band. This is achieved by suppressing 2.4 GHz probe response frames to station probe requests and by responding with 5 GHz probe response frames first.

Band select enables client radios that are capable of dual-band (2.4 and 5-GHz) operations to move to a less congested 5-GHz access point. The 2.4-GHz band is often congested.

65) D

Networking devices operate in two planes; the data plane and the control plane. The control plane maintains Layer 2 and Layer 3 forwarding mechanisms using the CPU. The data plane forwards traffic flows.

66) C

it can't be A because you're not going to choose TCP just because you have latency.

67) A

Reliability 255/255: When the input and output errors increase, they affect the reliability counter. This indicates how likely it is that a packet can be delivered or received successfully. Reliability is calculated like this: reliability = amount of packets / number of total frames. The value of 255 is the highest value meaning that the interface is very reliable at the moment. The calculation above is done every 5 minutes.

68) C is the right compressed address.

https://iplocation.io/ipv6-compress

69) D

70) C

71) B

A computer that hosts VMs requires specialized software called a hypervisor. The hypervisor emulates the computer's CPU, memory, hard disk, network and other hardware resources, creating a pool of resources that can be allocated to the individual VMs according to their specific requirements. The hypervisor can support multiple virtual hardware platforms that are isolated from each other, enabling VMs to run Linux and Windows Server OSes on the same physical host.

72) C

What DCA do:

-Dynamically manages channel assignments for an RF group.

-Evaluates the assignments on a per AP per radio basis

-Makes decisions using an RSSI based cost metric function which evaluates performance based on interference for each available channel.

-Dynamically adjusts the channel plan to maintain performance of individual radios.

-Actively manages 20/40/80/160 MHz bandwidth OBSS's.

To see DCA dynamically select channels, head over to the CLI on the controller and enter the debug command:

debug airwave-director channel enable.

Best answer is C relates more to Dynamic Channel Assignment DCA

https://packet6.com/configuring-cisco-rrm-dca-dynamic-channel-assignment/

Do not agree with D, which is more about Band Select and Band Direction but the feature does not alternate AP's automatically, this is wrong with the wording.

With the question specific to channel overlap, analyzing AP load with client associations, managing channel assignments per RF group.

https://www.cisco.com/c/en/us/td/docs/wireless/controller/technotes/8-3/b_RRM_White_Paper/b_RRM_White_Paper_chapter_0100.pdf

https://community.cisco.com/t5/wireless/how-to-deal-with-channel-overlapping-channel-interferences/td-p/2465741

73) C

Since private IP are used only on local network and can't be used over the internet (WAN0).

74) B

75) B

76) A

PC--A and PC-B are not in the same network. Switches send traffic in layer 2 and within the same VLA while routers route traffic to different subnet and at layer 3.

The key point is "verifying the IP addresses," it is done by router.

77) A

T1 link supports 1.544 Mbps, an E1 supports 2.048 Mbps, a T3 supports 43.7 Mbps, and an E3 connection supports 34.368 Mbps. Optical Carrier (OC) transmission rates are used to define the digital transmitting capacity of a fiber-optic network.

78) BD

79) D

Definitely not A as its physical when we are talking about cloud services.

B talks about access to a service but doesn't talk about topologies.

C feels like its referring to shared resources on a network between workstations and not on cloud.

80) D

"... the following list details some of the more common actions that a networking device does that fit into the data plane:

- De-encapsulating and re-encapsulating a packet in a data-link frame (routers, layer 3 switches).

- Adding or removing an 802.1Q trunking header (routers and switches).

- Matching an ethernet frame's destination MAC address to the MAC address table (layer 2 switches).

- Matching an IP packet's destination IP address to the IP routing table (routers, layer 3 switches).

- Encrypting the data and adding a new IP header (for VPN processing).

- Changing the source or destination IP address (for NAT) processing).

- Discarding a message due to a filter (ACLs, port security).

All the items in the list make up the data plane, because the data plane includes all actions done per message."

81) B

The trunk still forms with mismatched native VLANs and the traffic can actually flow between mismatched switches. But it is absolutely necessary that the native

VLANs on both ends of a trunk link match; otherwise, a native VLAN mismatch occurs, causing the two VLANs to effectively merge. For example, with the above configuration, SW1 would send untagged frames for VLAN 999. SW2 receives them but would think they are for VLAN 99 so we can say these two VLANs are merged.

82) D

When you enable Port Fast on the switch, spanning tree places ports in the forwarding state immediately, instead of going through the listening, learning, and forwarding states. If answer B did not say " when the switch is reloaded".

the question asks, what is the "primary" effect.

83) D

Enabling the Port Fast feature causes a switch or a trunk port to enter the STP forwarding-state immediately or upon a linkup event, thus bypassing the listening and learning states.

Note: To enable port fast on a trunk port you need the trunk keyword "spanning-tree port fast trunk"

1 day later and a little wiser then yesterday I can tell that I was wrong. BPDU Guard needs to be enabled for that, which is not the case.

84) A

WLAN Quality of Service (QoS) list:

• Platinum (voice)

• Gold (video)

- Silver (best effort) is the default value.

- Bronze (background)

Cisco Unified Wireless Network solution WLANs support four levels of QoS: Platinum/Voice, Gold/Video, Silver/Best Effort (default), and Bronze/Background.

Reference:

https://www.cisco.com/c/en/us/td/docs/wireless/controller/7-4/configuration/guides/consolidated/b_cg74_CONSOLIDATED/b_cg74_CONSOLIDATED_chapter_01010111.html

85) C

'0C:0E:15:1A' is the smallest MAC. It is assumed that priority is the same for all 4 switches.

$1A = (1 \times 16^1) + (10 \times 16^0) = 26 < A1 = (10 \times 16^1) + (1 \times 16^0) = 161$

$1A = 26 = 1 \times 16^1 + 10 \times 16^0$. but $22 = 2 \times 16^1 + 2 \times 16^0 = 34$. So $1A < 22$.

Least MAC value is selected in case of all the interface - Root Bridge priorities are same.

86) D

SW(config)#lldp tlv-select port-description

87) B

The lowest value of priority + MAC.

88) B

Because primary will decrement priority by 4096.

89) D

Because PC B in native VLAN. So ping will be failure.

90) C

In previous releases, whenever a FlexConnect access point disassociates from a controller, it moves to the standalone mode. The clients that are centrally switched are disassociated. However, the FlexConnect access point continues to serve locally switched clients. When the FlexConnect access point rejoins the controller (or a standby controller), all clients are disconnected and are authenticated again. This functionality has been enhanced and the connection between the clients and the FlexConnect access points are maintained intact and the clients experience seamless connectivity. When both the access point and the controller have the same configuration, the connection between the clients and APs is maintained.

When a FlexConnect access point can reach the controller (referred to as the connected mode), the controller assists in client authentication. When a FlexConnect access point cannot access the controller, the access point enters the standalone mode and authenticates clients by itself.

Reference:

https://www.cisco.com/c/en/us/td/docs/wireless/controller/7-4/configuration/guides/consolidated/b_cg74_CONSOLIDATED/
b_cg74_CONSOLIDATED_chapter_0100011
01.html

91) B

Reference:

https://www.cisco.com/E-Learning/bulk/public/tac/cim/cib/using_cisco_ios_software/cmdrefs/show_cdp_neighbors.htm#:~:text=Router%23-,show%20cdp%20neighbors,-Capability%20Codes%3A%20R

92) B

on

Mode that forces the LAN port to channel unconditionally. In the on mode, a usable EtherChannel exists only when a LAN port group in the on mode is connected to another LAN port group in the on mode.

Because ports configured in the on mode do not negotiate, there is no negotiation traffic between the ports. You cannot configure the on mode with an EtherChannel protocol. If one end uses the on mode, the other end must also.

auto

PAgP mode that places a LAN port into a passive negotiating state, in which the port responds to PAgP packets it receives but does not initiate PAgP negotiation. (Default)

desirable

PAgP mode that places a LAN port into an active negotiating state, in which the port initiates negotiations with other LAN ports by sending PAgP packets.

passive

LACP mode that places a port into a passive negotiating state, in which the port responds to LACP packets it receives but does not initiate LACP negotiation. (Default)

active

LACP mode that places a port into an active negotiating state, in which the port initiates negotiations with other ports by sending LACP packets.

93) B

Cisco Lightweight Access Point (LAP)

The Cisco LAP is part of the Cisco Unified Wireless Network architecture. A LAP is an AP that is designed to be connected to a wireless LAN (WLAN) controller (WLC). The LAP provides dual band support for IEEE 802.11a, 802.11b, and 802.11g and simultaneous air monitoring for dynamic, real-time radio frequency (RF) management. In addition, Cisco LAPs handle time-sensitive functions, such as Layer 2 encryption, that enable Cisco WLANs to securely support voice, video, and data applications.

APs are "lightweight," which means that they cannot act independently of a wireless LAN controller (WLC). The WLC manages the AP configurations and firmware. The APs are "zero touch" deployed, and individual configuration of APs is not necessary. The APs are also lightweight in the sense that they handle only real-time MAC functionality. The APs leave all the non-real-time MAC functionality to be processed by the WLC. This architecture is referred to as the "split MAC" architecture.

A Lightweight Access Point (LAP) is an AP that is designed to be connected to a wireless LAN (WLAN) controller (WLC). APs are "lightweight", which means that they cannot act independently of a wireless LAN controller (WLC). The WLC manages the AP configurations and firmware. The APs are "zero touch" deployed, and individual configuration of APs is not necessary.

Reference:

https://www.cisco.com/c/en/us/support/docs/wireless/aironet-1200-series/70278-lap-faq.html

94) CD

Editing WLAN SSID or Profile Name for WLANs (GUI)

Procedure

Step 1

Choose WLANs to open the WLANs page.

This page lists all of the WLANs currently configured on the controller. For each WLAN, you can see its WLAN ID, profile name, type, SSID, status, and security policies.

The total number of WLANs appears in the upper right-hand corner of the page. If the list of WLANs spans multiple pages, you can access these pages by clicking the page number links.

Step 2

To edit a WLAN profile or SSID, click the WLAN ID link in the WLANs > Edit page.

In the Profile Name field, edit the WLAN profile name.

In the WLAN SSID field, edit the WLAN SSID.

Step 3

Click Apply to commit your changes.

Step 4

Click Save Configuration to save your changes.

95) C

Specifies the delay time in seconds for LLDP to initialize on any interface.

The range is 1 to 10 seconds; the default is 2 seconds.

96) D

Transparent—VTP transparent switches do not participate in VTP. A VTP transparent switch does not advertise its VLAN configuration and does not synchronize its VLAN configuration based on received advertisements, but transparent switches do forward VTP advertisements that they receive out their trunk ports in VTP Version 2.

The VTP mode of SW2 is transparent so it only forwards the VTP updates it receives to its trunk links without processing them.

Reference:

https://www.cisco.com/c/en/us/support/docs/lan-switching/vtp/10558-21.html

97) B

Both partner and local routers cannot be in the same passive mode for a link to form. The question is asking "what mode are YOU on". Well since you are able to see your partner information you would be in "active mode". Weather you partner is on "active" or "passive" doesn't matter, as long as you are active you can pull neighbors information.

With LACP, at least one side must be active. So if the SW1 neighbor is passive, SW1 must be active.

98) D

Dynamic Auto — Makes the Ethernet port willing to convert the link to a trunk link. The port becomes a trunk port if the neighboring port is set to trunk or dynamic desirable mode. This is the default mode for some switchports.

Dynamic Desirable — Makes the port actively attempt to convert the link to a trunk link. The port becomes a trunk port if the neighboring Ethernet port is set to trunk, dynamic desirable or dynamic auto mode.

99) B

"Untagged traffic from the device attached to the Cisco IP Phone passes through the phone unchanged, regardless of the trust state of the access port on the phone"

Reference:

https://www.cisco.com/c/en/us/td/docs/switches/lan/catalyst2960/software/release/12-2_40_se/configuration/guide/scg/swvoip.pdf

100) A

Selecting the proper WiFi channel can significantly improve your WiFi coverage and performance. In the 2.4 GHz band, 1, 6, and 11 are the only non-overlapping channels. Selecting one or more of these channels is an important part of setting up your network correctly.

101) D

Native VLAN: The native VLAN is the one into which untagged traffic will be put when it's received on a trunk port. This makes it possible for your VLAN to support legacy devices or devices that don't tag their traffic like some wireless access points and simply network attached devices.

102) CD

We can answer this by discarding incorrect answers we need to use an open standard IE LACP.

The option "A" is discarded: PAgP configuration.

The option "B" is discarded: manual configuration ("On" mode).

The option "C" is configuration that LACP uses.

The option "D" is configuration that LACP uses.

The option "E" is discarded: It is configuration of trunk mode, not Etherchannel.

103) AC

Desirable/Auto (PAGP)

Active/Passive (LACP)

104) B

Since the native VLAN is not referenced, we can safely assume it is VLAN1 (native defaulting to the default VLAN if not configured) and the untagged data PC traffic passes through the phone unchanged. If the data traffic was tagged, we would likely have more details here such as cos value or trust with the switchport priority.

105) C

Untagged and native VLAN go together, so VLAN 5. However, 'switchport mode trunk' and switchport access VALN 11', not good.

106) A

#lldp run - Golably Enable.

#no lldp run - Globally Disable.

#lldp Recieve -To receive LLDP packets.

#lldp Transmit - To transmit LLDP packets.

Link Layer Discovery Protocol (LLDP) is an industry standard protocol that allows devices to advertise, and discover connected devices, and their capabilities.

(Same as CDP of Cisco). To enable it on Cisco devices, we have to use this command under global configuration mode:

Sw(config)# lldp run

107) D

☞ lldp holdtime seconds: Specify the amount of time a receiving device should hold the information from your device before discarding it lldp reinit delay:

Specify the delay time in seconds for LLDP to initialize on an interface.

☞ lldp timer rate: Set the sending frequency of LLDP updates in seconds

Reference:

https://www.cisco.com/c/en/us/td/docs/switches/lan/catalyst3560/software/release/12-2_55_se/configuration/guide/3560_scg/swlldp.html

108) B

If a neighbor has no IP address on an interface enabled with Cisco Discovery Protocol, the IP address of another interface will be updated as IP address for the non-IP address interface.

Reference:
https://www.cisco.com/c/en/us/td/docs/ios-xml/ios/cdp/configuration/15-mt/cdp-15-mt-book/nm-cdp-discover.html

109) A

The LACP is Link Aggregation Control Protocol. LACP is an open protocol, published under the 802.3ad.

The modes of LACP are active, passive or on. The side configured as "passive" will waiting the other side that should an Active for the Etherchannel to be established.

PAgP is Port-Aggregation Protocol. It is Cisco proprietary protocol. The mode is On, Desirable or Auto. Desirable " Auto will establish an EtherChannel.

An example of how to configure an Etherchannel:

SwitchFormula1>enable -

SwitchFormula1#configure terminal

SwitchFormula1(config)# interface range f0/5 -14

SwitchFormula1(config-if-range)# channel-group 13 mode ?

active Enable LACP unconditionally

auto Enable PAgP only if a PAgP device is detected

desirable Enable PAgP unconditionally

on Enable Etherchannel only

passive Enable LACP only if a LACP device is detected.

Actually, a good question since this verifies the knowledge of how LACP works - remember a channel in Passive "wants" to be part of a channel but will sit and wait and only bind if the other end is "Active". I think of "Passive" as follow the leader and "active" as the "do what I say" bully config.

110) A

Cisco switches always have VLAN 1 as the default VLAN, which is needed for many protocols communication between switches like spanning-tree protocol for instance.

You can't change or even delete the default VLAN, it is mandatory.

The native VLAN is the only VLAN which is not tagged in a trunk, in other words, native VLAN frames are transmitted unchanged.

Reference:

https://community.cisco.com/t5/switching/
what-is-difference-between-default-vlan-
and-native-vlan/td-p/2095204

111) BC

Deafult Vlans

1

1002

1003

1004

1005

VLAN 1 is a system default VLAN, you can use this VLAN but you cannot delete it. By default, VLAN 1 is use for every port on the switch.

Standard VLAN range from 1002-1005 it's Cisco default for FDDI and Token Ring. You cannot delete VLANs 1002-1005. Mostly we don't use VLAN in this range.

112) AC

The information contained in Cisco Discovery Protocol advertisements varies based on the type of device and the installed version of the operating system. Some of the information that Cisco Discovery Protocol can learn includes:

Cisco IOS version running on Cisco devices.

Hardware platform of devices.

IP addresses of interfaces on devices.

Locally connected devices advertising Cisco Discovery Protocol.

Interfaces active on Cisco devices, including encapsulation type.

Hostname.

Duplex setting.

***VLAN Trunking Protocol (VTP) domain.

***Native VLAN.

113) AE

In order of importance security policies and load balancing should be at the top of the list. POE would likely be third in line mainly because this would be a budgeted consideration and not necessarily an immediate post-deployment task requirement.

Reference:

https://www.cisco.com/c/en/us/td/docs/wireless/controller/technotes/8-6/b_Cisco_Wireless_LAN_Controller_Configuration_Best_Practices.html#concept_574CD7840A6C4DBBA7CF465C2C90304B

114) B

SW1 trunk native vlan 10 commands will drop the tag from any Vlan 10 traffic and send it out to SW2 without a tag.

SW2 see's untagged traffic from SW1 and applies it to Native Vlan 100.

Since SW-1 is configured native VLAN is VLAN10, so traffic coming out of VLAN-10 is untagged, & goes directly to SW-2 Native VLAN: VLAN100, due to VLAN mismatch.

115) DE

Answer D is used to 'actively negotiate' for PAGP and answer E is used to 'actively negotiate for LACP.

116) D

TTL is Layer 3 which won't apply in this scenario. Thus, answer A is wrong.

117) AD

"All switches in a VTP domain must have the same domain name, but they do not need to run the same VTP version".

Reference:

https://www.cisco.com/c/en/us/td/docs/switches/lan/catalyst3560/software/release/12-2_52_se/configuration/guide/3560scg/swvtp.html#wp1107364

118) D

" The port that receives the best BPDU on a bridge is the root port "

Reference:

https://www.cisco.com/c/en/us/support/docs/lan-switching/spanning-tree-protocol/24062-146.html#:~:text=The%20port%20that%20receives%20the,ones%20any%20other%20bridge%20sends.

119) B

This is an STP-related question.

Reference:

https://www.cisco.com/c/m/en_us/techdo
c/dc/reference/cli/n5k/commands/spannin
g-tree-port-priority.html

120) A

This is pure product placement.

Not C Because the option doesn't specifically say from Cisco router, switches, etc.

Not D because it does operate on the data-link layer but Not on the physical layer.

However, option A is the first thing we learn about CDP, that it's Cisco proprietary.

Practice Test II

1) What are two reasons a network administrator would use CDP?

(Choose two.)

A. to verify the type of cable interconnecting two devices.

B. to determine the status of network services on a remote device.

C. to obtain VLAN information from directly connected switches.

D. to verify Layer 2 connectivity between two devices when Layer 3 fails.

E. to obtain the IP address of a connected device in order to telnet to the device.

F. to determine the status of the routing protocols between directly connected routers.

2) What are two benefits of using VTP in a switching environment?

(Choose two.)

A. It allows switches to read frame tags.

B. It allows ports to be assigned to VLANs automatically.

C. It maintains VLAN consistency across a switched network.

D. It allows frames from multiple VLANs to use a single interface.

E. It allows VLAN information to be automatically propagated throughout the switching environment.

3) Which three statements are typical characteristics of VLAN arrangements? (Choose three.)

A. A new switch has no VLANs configured.

B. Connectivity between VLANs requires a Layer 3 device.

C. VLANs typically decrease the number of collision domains.

D. Each VLAN uses a separate address space.

E. A switch maintains a separate bridging table for each VLAN.

F. VLANs cannot span multiple switches.

4) On a corporate network, hosts on the same VLAN can communicate with each other, but they are unable to communicate with hosts on different VLANs.

What is needed to allow communication between the VLANs?

A. a router with sub interfaces configured on the physical interface that is connected to the switch.

B. a router with an IP address on the physical interface connected to the switch.

C. a switch with an access link that is configured between the switches.

D. a switch with a trunk link that is configured between the switches.

5) Which statement about LLDP is true?

A. It is a Cisco proprietary protocol.

B. It is configured in global configuration mode.

C. The LLDP update frequency is a fixed value.

D. It runs over the transport layer.

6) What is a function of Wireless LAN Controller?

A. register with a single access point that controls traffic between wired and wireless endpoints.

B. use SSIDs to distinguish between wireless clients.

C. send LWAPP packets to access points.

D. monitor activity on wireless and wired LANs.

7) Which technology is used to improve web traffic performance by proxy caching?

A. WSA.

B. Firepower.

C. ASA.

D. FireSIGHT.

8) What criteria is used first during the root port selection process?

A. local port ID.

B. lowest path cost to the root bridge.

C. lowest neighbor's bridge ID.

D. lowest neighbor's port ID.

9) Which statement about VLAN configuration is true?

A. The switch must be in VTP server or transparent mode before you can configure a VLAN.

B. The switch must be in config-vlan mode before you configure an extended VLAN.

C. Dynamic inter-VLAN routing is supported on VLAN2 through VLAN 4064.

D. A switch in VTP transparent mode save the VLAN databases to the running configuration only.

10) Refer to the exhibit.

What two conclusions should be made about this configuration? (Choose two.)

```
SW1#show spanning-tree vlan 30

VLAN0030
Spanning tree enabled protocol rstp
Root ID        Priority          32798
               Address           0025.63e9.c800
               Cost              19
               Port              1 (FastEthernet 2/1)
               Hello Time        2 sec
               Max Age           30 sec
               Forward Delay     20 sec

[Output suppressed]
```

A. The root port is FastEthernet 2/1

B. The designated port is FastEthernet 2/1

C. The spanning-tree mode is PVST+

D. This is a root bridge

E. The spanning-tree mode is Rapid PVST+

11) A network engineer must create a diagram of a multivendor network.

Which command must be configured on the Cisco devices so that the topology of the network is allowed to be mapped?

A. Device(config)#lldp run

B. Device(config)#cdp run

C. Device(config-if)#cdp enable

D.Device(config)#flow-sampler-map topology

12) How do AAA operations compare regarding user identification, user services, and access control?

A. Authorization provides access control, and authentication tracks user services.

B. Authentication identifies users, and accounting tracks user services.

C. Accounting tracks user services, and authentication provides access control.

D. Authorization identifies users, and authentication provides access control.

13) What is the difference between RADIUS and TACACS+?

A. RADIUS logs all commands that are entered by the administrator, but TACACS+ logs only start, stop, and interim commands.

B. TACACS+ separates authentication and authorization, and RADIUS merges them.

C. TACACS+ encrypts only password information, and RADIUS encrypts the entire payload.

D. RADIUS is most appropriate for dial authentication, but TACACS+ can be used for multiple types of authentications.

14) What is a difference between local AP mode and FlexConnect AP mode?

A. Local AP mode creates two CAPWAP tunnels per AP to the WLC.

B. Local AP mode causes the AP to behave as if it were an autonomous AP.

C. FlexConnect AP mode fails to function if the AP loses connectivity with the WLC.

D. FlexConnect AP mode bridges the traffic from the AP to the WLC when local switching is configured.

15) The SW1 interface g0/1 is in the down/down state.

What are two reasons for the interface condition? (Choose two.)

A. There is a protocol mismatch.

B. There is a duplex mismatch.

C. The interface is shut down.

D. The interface is error-disabled.

E. There is a speed mismatch.

16) How will Link Aggregation be implemented on a Cisco Wireless LAN Controller?

A. The EtherChannel must be configured in "mode active".

B. When enabled, the WLC bandwidth drops to 500 Mbps.

C. To pass client traffic, two or more ports must be configured.

D. One functional physical port is needed to pass client traffic.

17) Which two conditions must be met before SSH operates normally on a Cisco IOS switch? (Choose two.)

A. IP routing must be enabled on the switch.

B. A console password must be configured on the switch.

C. Telnet must be disabled on the switch.

D. The switch must be running a k9 (crypto) IOS image.

E. The ip domain-name command must be configured on the switch.

18)

```
Atlanta#conf t
Enter configuration commands, one per line. End with CNTL/Z.
Atlanta(config)#aaa new-model
Atlanta(config)#aaa authentication login default local
Atlanta(config)#line vty 0 4
Atlanta(config-line)#login authentication default
Atlanta(config-line)#exit
Atlanta(config)#username ciscoadmin password adminadmin123
Atlanta(config)#username ciscoadmin privilege 15
Atlanta(config)#enable password cisco123
Atlanta(config)#enable secret testing1234
Atlanta(config)#end
```

Refer to the exhibit. Which password must an engineer use to enter the enable mode?

A. adminadmin123

B. cisco123

C. default

D. testing1234

19) Which state does the switch port move to when PortFast is enabled?

A. blocking.

B. listening.

C. learning.

D. forwarding.

20) Which protocol prompts the Wireless LAN Controller to generate its own local web administration SSL certificate for GUI access?

A. RADIUS

B. HTTPS

C. TACACS+

D. HTTP

21) An engineer must configure interswitch VLAN communication between a Cisco switch and a third-party switch.

Which action should be taken?

A. configure DSCP

B. configure IEEE 802.1q

C. configure ISL

D. configure IEEE 802.1p

22) An engineer requires a switch interface to actively attempt to establish a trunk link with a neighbor switch.

What command must be configured?

A. switchport mode trunk.

B. switchport mode dynamic desirable.

C. switchport no negotiate.

D. switchport mode dynamic auto.

23) Refer to the exhibit. After the election process, what is the root bridge in the HQ LAN?

Switch 1: 0C:E0:38:81:32:58 -

Switch 2: 0C:0E:15:22:1A:61 -

Switch 3: 0C:0E:15:1D:3C:9A -

Switch 4: 0C:E0:19:A1:4D:16 –

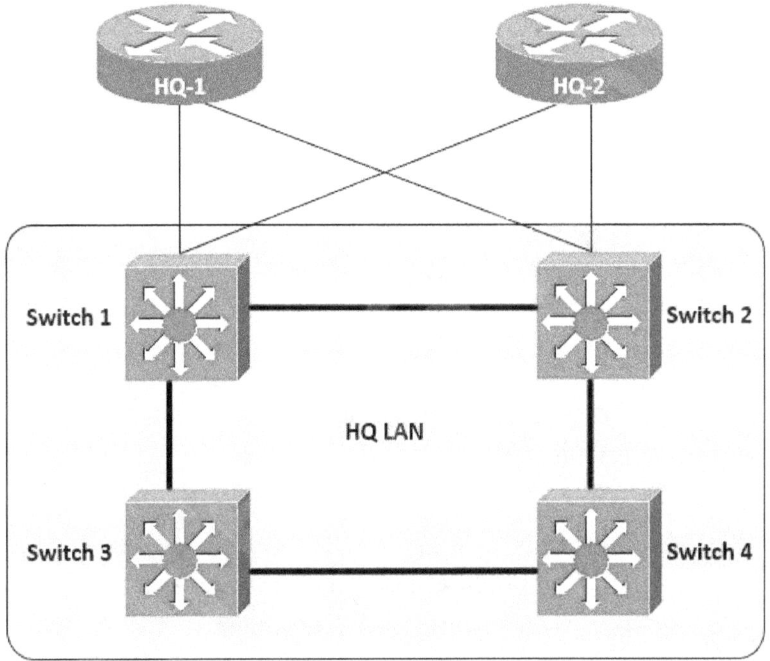

A. Switch 1

B. Switch 2

C. Switch 3

D. Switch 4

24) An engineer must establish a trunk link between two switches. The neighboring switch is set to trunk or desirable mode.

What action should be taken?

A. configure switchport no negotiate.

B. configure switchport mode dynamic desirable.

C. configure switchport mode dynamic auto.

D. configure switchport trunk dynamic desirable.

25) Which spanning-tree enhancement avoids the learning and listening states and immediately places ports in the forwarding state?

A. BPDUfilter

B. PortFast

C. Backbonefast

D. BPDUguard

26) How does the dynamically-learned MAC address feature function?

A. The CAM table is empty until ingress traffic arrives at each port.

B. Switches dynamically learn MAC addresses of each connecting CAM table.

C. The ports are restricted and learn up to a maximum of 10 dynamically-learned addresses.

D. It requires a minimum number of secure MAC addresses to be filled dynamically.

27) When using Rapid PVST+, which command guarantees the switch is always the root bridge for VLAN 200?

A. spanning-tree vlan 200 priority 614440

B. spanning-tree vlan 200 priority 0

C. spanning-tree vlan 200 root primaries

D. spanning-tree vlan 200 priority 38813258

28)

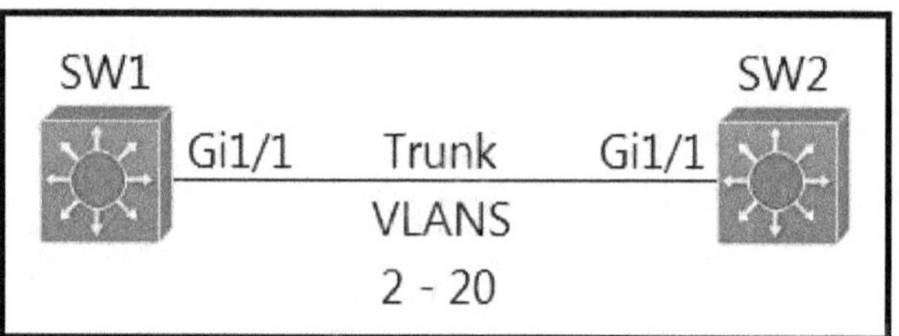

Refer to the exhibit. Which command must be executed for Gi1/1 on SW1 to passively become a trunk port if Gi1/1 on SW2 is configured in desirable or trunk mode?

A. switchport mode dynamic auto.

B. switchport mode dot1-tunnel.

C. switchport mode dynamic desirable.

D. switchport mode trunk.

29)

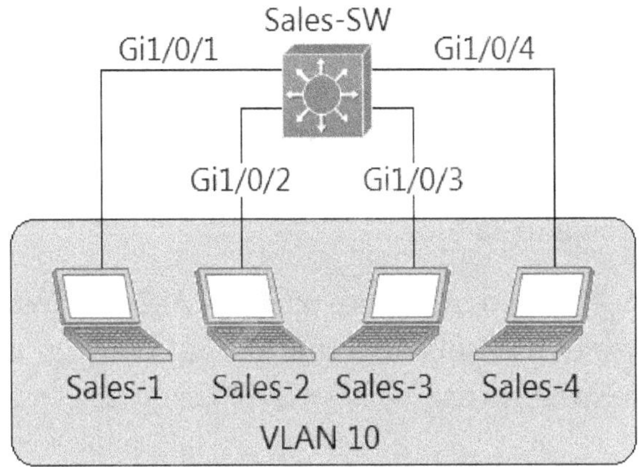

Refer to the exhibit. The entire contents or the MAC address table are shown. Sales-4 sends a data frame to Sales-1.

Sales-SW#show mac-address-table
Mac Address Table

VLAN	MAC Address	Type	Ports
10	000c.8590.bb7d	DYNAMIC	Gi1/0/1
10	3939.1170.1bb7	DYNAMIC	Gi1/0/2
10	00d0.d3b6.957c	DYNAMIC	Gi1/0/3

Sales-SW#

What does the switch do as it receives the frame from Sales-4?

A. Map the Layer 2 MAC address to the Layer 3 IP address and forward the frame.

B. Insert the source MAC address and port into the forwarding table and forward the frame to Sales-1.

C. Perform a lookup in the MAC address table and discard the frame due to a missing entry.

D. Flood the frame out of all ports except on the port where Sales-1 is connected.

30)

SW10

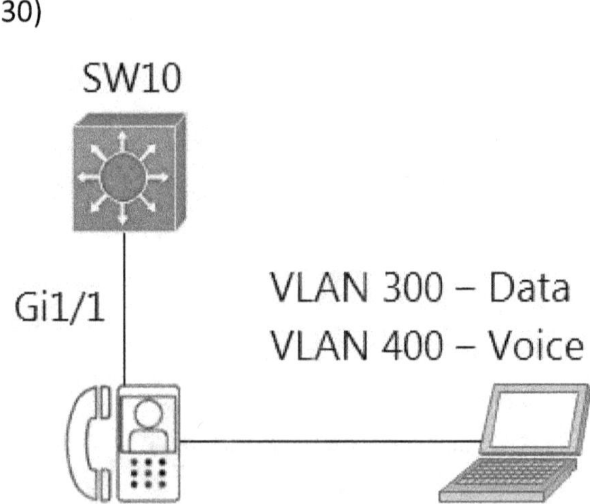

Refer to the exhibit. An engineer must configure GigabitEthernet1/1 to accommodate voice and data traffic.

Which configuration accomplishes this task?

A. interface gigabitethernet1/1 switchport mode access switchport access vlan 300 switchport voice vlan 400.

B. interface gigabitethernet1/1 switchport mode trunk switchport trunk vlan 300 switchport trunk vlan 400.

C. interface gigabitethernet1/1 switchport mode access switchport voice vlan 300 switchport access vlan 400.

D. interface gigabitethernet1/1 switchport mode trunk switchport trunk vlan 300 switchport voice vlan 400.

31) An engineer needs to add an old switch back into a network. To prevent the switch from corrupting the VLAN database, with action must be taken?

A. Add the switch in the VTP domain with a lower revision number.

B. Add the switch in the VTP domain with a higher revision number.

C. Add the switch with DTP set to dynamic desirable.

D. Add the switch with DTP set to desirable.

32) Which technology prevents client devices from arbitrarily connecting to the network without state remediation?

A. 802.11n

B. 802.1x

C. MAC Authentication Bypass

D. IP Source Guard

33) Which protocol does an access point use to draw power from a connected switch?

A. Internet Group Management Protocol.

B. Cisco Discovery Protocol.

C. Adaptive Wireless Path Protocol.

D. Neighbor Discovery Protocol.

34) An administrator must secure the WLC from receiving spoofed association requests. Which steps must be taken to configure the WLC to restrict the requests and force the user to wait 10 ms to retry an association request?

A. Enable MAC filtering and set the SA Query timeout to 10.

B. Enable 802.1x Layer 2 security and set the Comeback timer to 10.

C. Enable Security Association Teardown Protection and set the SA Query timeout to 10.

D. Enable the Protected Management Frame service and set the Comeback timer to 10.

35)

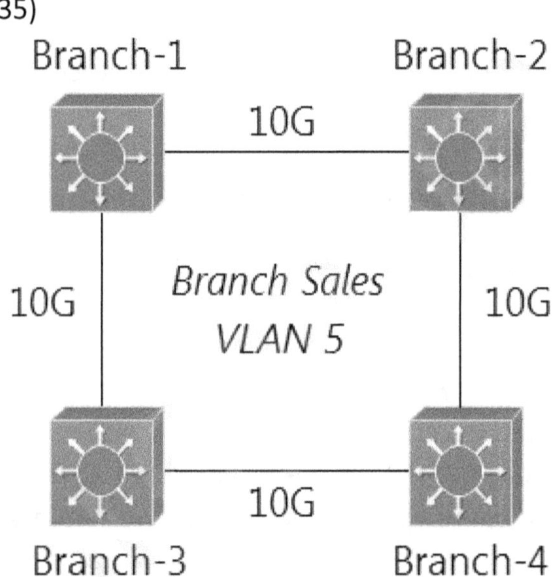

Refer to the exhibit. Only four switches are participating in the VLAN spanning-tree process.

Branch-1: priority 614440 -

Branch-2: priority 39391170 -

Branch-3: priority 0 -

Branch-4: root primary -

Which switch becomes the permanent root bridge for VLAN 5?

A. Branch-1

B. Branch-2

C. Branch-3

D. Branch-4

36) An engineer must configure traffic for a VLAN that is untagged by the switch as it crosses a trunk link. Which command should be used?

A. switchport trunk encapsulation dot1q

B. switchport trunk allowed vlan 10

C. switchport mode trunk

D. switchport trunk native vlan 10

37) What are two benefits of using the PortFast feature? (Choose two.)

A. Enabled interfaces are automatically placed in listening state.

B. Enabled interfaces wait 50 seconds before they move to the forwarding state.

C. Enabled interfaces never generate topology change notifications.

D. Enabled interfaces come up and move to the forwarding state immediately.

E. Enabled interfaces that move to the learning state generate switch topology change notifications.

38) What is the benefit of configuring PortFast on an interface?

A. The frames entering the interface are marked with the higher priority and then processed faster by a switch.

B. After the cable is connected, the interface is available faster to send and receive user data.

C. Real-time voice and video frames entering the interface are processed faster.

D. After the cable is connected, the interface uses the fastest speed setting available for that cable type.

39) Why does a switch flood a frame to all ports?

A. The frame has zero destination MAC addresses.

B. The destination MAC address of the frame is unknown.

C. The source MAC address of the frame is unknown

D. The source and destination MAC addresses of the frame are the same.

40) An engineer configures interface Gi1/0 on the company PE router to connect to an ISP. Neighbor discovery is disabled.

```
interface Gi1/0
description HQ_DC3992-38488
duplex full
speed 100
negotiation auto
lldp transmit
lldp receive
```

Which action is necessary to complete the configuration if the ISP uses third-party network devices?

A. Disable autonegotiation.

B. Enable LLDP globally.

C. Enable LLDP-MED on the ISP device.

D. Disable Cisco Discovery Protocol on the interface.

41) Which access point mode relies on a centralized controller for management, roaming, and SSID configuration?

A. lightweight mode.

B. autonomous mode.

C. bridge mode.

D. repeater mode.

42)

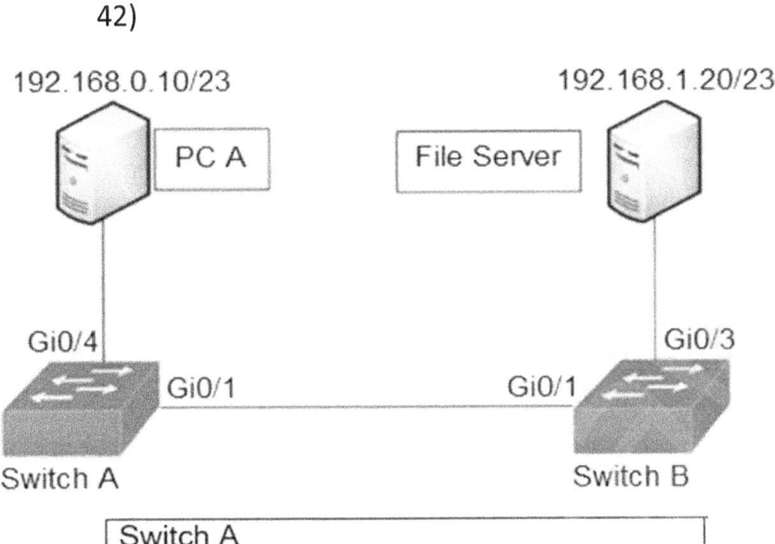


```
Switch A
Vlan 10, 11, 12, 13

interface GigabitEthernet0/1
 switchport mode trunk
 switchport trunk allowed vlan 10-12
!
interface GigabitEthernet0/4
 switchport access vlan 13
 switchport mode access
```

```
Switch B
Vlan 10, 11, 12, 13

interface GigabitEthernet0/1
switchport mode trunk
!
interface GigabitEthernet0/3
  switchport access vlan 13
  switchport mode access
```

Refer to the exhibit. A network engineer must configure communication between PC A and the File Server.

To prevent interruption for any other communications, which command must be configured?

A. switchport trunck allowed vlan 12

B. switchport trunck allowed vlan none

C. switchport trunck allowed vlan add 13

D. switchport trunck allowed vlan remove 10-11

43)

```
switch(config)#interface gigabitEthernet 1/11

switch(config-if)#switchport mode access

switch(config-if)#spanning-tree portfast

switch(config-if)#spanning-tree bpduguard enable
```

Refer to the exhibit. What is the result if Gig1/11 receives an STP BPDU?

A. The port transitions to STP blocking.

B. The port immediately transitions to STP forwarding.

C. The port goes into error-disable state.

D. The port transitions to the root port.

44) Which access layer threat-mitigation technique provides security based on identity?

A. Dynamic ARP Inspection.

B. DHCP snooping.

C. 802.1x.

D. using a non-default native VLAN.

45) Refer to the exhibit. Which configuration issue is preventing the OSPF neighbor relationship from being established between the two routers?

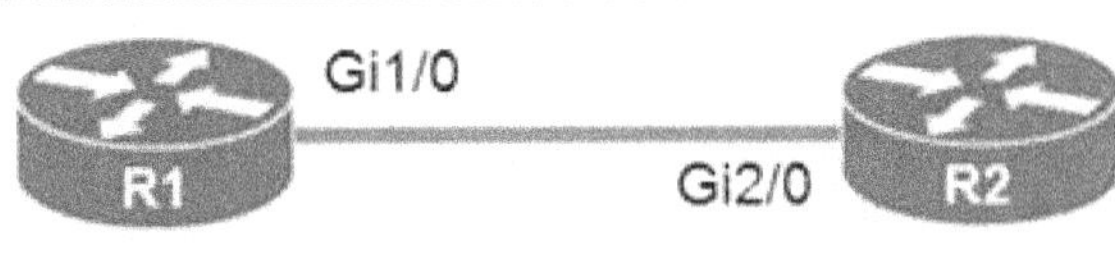


```
R1#show running-config
Building configuration...
!
interface GigabitEthernet1/0
 mtu 1600
 ip address 192.168.0.1 255.255.255.252
 negotiation auto
!
router ospf 1
 router-id 1.1.1.1
 passive-interface default
 no passive-interface GigabitEthernet1/0
 network 192.168.0.1 0.0.0.0 area 0
!
R2#show running-config
Building configuration...
!
interface GigabitEthernet2/0
 ip address 192.168.0.2 255.255.255.252
 negotiation auto
!
router ospf 1
 router-id 2.2.2.2
 passive-interface default
 no passive-interface GigabitEthernet2/0
 network 192.168.0.2 0.0.0.0 area 0
```

A. R1 has an incorrect network command for interface Gi1/0.

B. R2 should have its network command in area 1.

C. R1 interface Gi1/0 has a larger MTU size.

D. R2 is using the passive-interface default command.

46) Refer to the exhibit. Router R1 is running three different routing protocols. Which route characteristic is used by the router to forward the packet that it receives for destination IP 172.16.32.1?

```
R1# show ip route
....
D       172.16.32.0/27      [90/2888597172] via 20.1.1.1
O       172.16.32.0/19      [110/292094] via 20.1.1.10
R       172.16.32.0/24      [120/2] via 20.1.1.3
```

A. longest prefix

B. administrative distance

C. cost

D. metric

47) Refer to the exhibit. Router R1 Fa0/0 cannot ping router R3 Fa0/1. Which action must be taken in router R1 to help resolve the configuration issue?

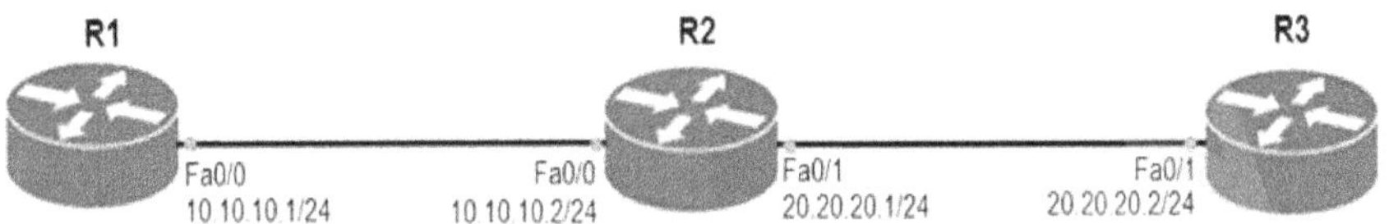


```
R1#show ip route
Codes: C - connected, S - static, R - RIP, M - mobile, B - BGP
       D - EIGRP, EX - EIGRP external, O - OSPF, IA - OSPF inter area
       N1 - OSPF NSSA external type 1, N2 - OSPF NSSA external type 2
       E1 - OSPF external type 1, E2 - OSPF external type 2
       i - IS-IS, su - IS-IS summary, L1 - IS-IS level-1, L2 - IS-IS level-2
       ia - IS-IS inter area, * - candidate default, U - per-user static route
       o - DDR, P - periodic downloaded static route

Gateway of last resort is not set

     10.0.0.0/24 is subnettted, 1 subnets
C        10.10.10.0 is directly connected, FastEthernet0/0
```

```
R2#show ip route
Codes: C - connected, S - static, R - RIP, M - mobile, B - BGP
       D - EIGRP, EX - EIGRP external, 0 - OSPF, IA - OSPF inter area
       N1 - OSPF NSSA external type 1, N2 - OSPF NSSA external type 2
       E1 - OSPF external type 1, E2 - OSPF external type 2
       i - IS-IS, su - IS-IS summary, L1 - IS-IS level-1, L2 - IS-IS level-2
       ia - IS-IS inter area, * - candidate default, U - per-user static route
       o - DDR, P - periodic downloaded static route

Gateway of last resort is not set

        20.0.0.0/24 is subnettted, 1 subnets
C          20.20.20.0 is directly connected, FastEthernet0/1
        10.0.0.0/24 is subnettted, 1 subnets
C          10.10.10.0 is directly connected, FastEthernet0/0
```

```
R3#show ip route
Codes: C - connected, S - static, R - RIP, M - mobile, B - BGP
       D - EIGRP, EX - EIGRP external, 0 - OSPF, IA - OSPF inter area
       N1 - OSPF NSSA external type 1, N2 - OSPF NSSA external type 2
       E1 - OSPF external type 1, E2 - OSPF external type 2
       i - IS-IS, su - IS-IS summary, L1 - IS-IS level-1, L2 - IS-IS level-2
       ia - IS-IS inter area, * - candidate default, U - per-user static route
       o - DDR, P - periodic downloaded static route

Gateway of last resort is not set

        20.0.0.0/24 is subnettted, 1 subnets
C          20.20.20.0 is directly connected, FastEthernet0/1
        10.0.0.0/24 is subnettted, 1 subnets
S          10.10.10.0 (1/0) via 20.20.20.1
```

A. set the default gateway as 20.20.20.2

B. configure a static route with Fa0/1 as the egress interface to reach the 20.20.2.0/24 network

C. configure a static route with 10.10.10.2 as the next hop to reach the 20.20.20.0/24 network

D. set the default network as 20.20.20.0/24

48) By default, how does EIGRP determine the metric of a route for the routing table?

A. It uses the bandwidth and delay values of the path to calculate the route metric.

B. It uses a default metric of 10 for all routes that are learned by the router.

C. It counts the number of hops between the receiving and destination routers and uses that value as the metric.

D. It uses a reference bandwidth and the actual bandwidth of the connected link to calculate the route metric.

49) Router R1 must send all traffic without a matching routing-table entry to 192.168.1.1. Which configuration accomplishes this task?

A. R1# onfig t R1(config)#ip routing R1(config)#ip route default-route 192.168.1.1

B. R1# onfig t R1(config)#ip routing R1(config)#ip route 192.168.1.1 0.0.0.0 0.0.0.0

C. R1# onfig t R1(config)#ip routing R1(config)#ip route 0.0.0.0 0.0.0.0 192.168.1.1

D. R1# onfig t R1(config)#ip routing R1(config)#ip default-gateway 192.168.1.1

50) A packet is destined for 10.10.1.22.

Which static route does the router choose to forward the packet?

A. ip route 10.10.1.0 255.255.255.240
10.10.255.1

B. ip route 10.10.1.20 255.255.255.252
10.10.255.1

C. ip route 10.10.1.16 255.255.255.252
10.10.255.1

D. ip route 10.10.1.20 255.255.255.254
10.10.255.1

51)

EIGRP: 192.168.12.0/24
RIP: 192.168.12.0/27
OSPF: 192.168.12.0/28

Refer to the exhibit. How does the router manage traffic to 192.168.12.16?

A. It chooses the EIGRP route because it has the lowest administrative distance.

B. It load-balances traffic between all three routes.

C. It chooses the OSPF route because it has the longest prefix inclusive of the destination address.

D. It selects the RIP route because it has the longest prefix inclusive of the destination address.

52) What are two reasons for an engineer to configure a floating static route? (Choose two.)

A. to enable fallback static routing when the dynamic routing protocol fails.

B. to route traffic differently based on the source IP of the packet.

C. to automatically route traffic on a secondary path when the primary path goes down.

D. to support load balancing via static routing.

E. to control the return path of traffic that is sent from the router.

53)

```
R1# show ip route

D       192.168.10.0/24     [90/2679326] via 192.168.1.1
R       192.168.10.0/27     [120/3] via 192.168.1.2
O       192.168.10.0/23     [110/2] via 192.168.1.3
i L1    192.168.10.0/13     [115/30] via 192.168.1.4
```

Refer to the exhibit. How does router R1 handle traffic to 192.168.10.16?

A. It selects the IS-IS route because it has the shortest prefix inclusive of the destination address.

B. It selects the RIP route because it has the longest prefix inclusive of the destination address.

C. It selects the OSPF route because it has the lowest cost.

D. It selects the EIGRP route because it has the lowest administrative distance.

54)

```
IBGP route 10.0.0.0/30
RIP route 10.0.0.0/30
OSPF route 10.0.0.0/16
OSPF route 10.0.0.0/30
EIGRP route 10.0.0.1/32
```

Refer to the exhibit. A router received these five routes from different routing information sources.

Which two routes does the router install in its routing table?

(Choose two.)

A. OSPF route 10.0.0.0/30

B. IBGP route 10.0.0.0/30

C. OSPF route 10.0.0.0/16

D. EIGRP route 10.0.0.1/32

E. RIP route 10.0.0.0/30

55)

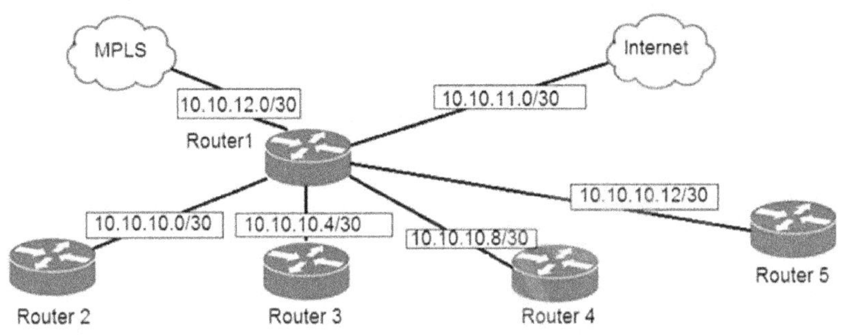


```
Router1#show ip route
Gateway of last resort is 10.10.11.2 to network 0.0.0.0
        209.165.200.0/27 is subnetted, 1 subnets
B          209.165.200.224 [20/0] via 10.10.12.2, 03:22:14
        209.165.201.0/27 is subnetted, 1 subnets
B          209.165.201.0 [20/0] via 10.10.12.2, 02:26:33
        209.165.202.0/27 is subnetted, 1 subnets
B          209.165.202.128 [20/0] via 10.10.12.2, 02:26:03
        10.0.0.0/8 is variably subnetted, 10 subnets, 4 masks
O          10.10.13.0/25 [110/2] via 10.10.10.1, 00:00:04, GigabitEthernet0/0
O          10.10.13.128/28 [110/2] via 10.10.10.5, 00:00:12, GigabitEthernet0/1
O          10.10.13.144/28 [110/2] via 10.10.10.9, 00:01:57, GigabitEthernet0/2
O          10.10.13.160/29 [110/2] via 10.10.10.5, 00:00:12, GigabitEthernet0/1
O          10.10.13.208/29 [110/2] via 10.10.10.13, 00:01:57, GigabitEthernet0/3
S*      0.0.0.0/0 [1/0] via 10.10.11.2
```

Refer to the exhibit. To which device does Router1 send packets that are destined to host 10.10.13.165?

A. Router2

B. Router3

C. Router4

D. Router5

56) R1 has learned route 10.10.10.0/24 via numerous routing protocols. Which route is installed?

A. route with the next hop that has the highest IP.

B. route with the lowest cost.

C. route with the lowest administrative distance.

D. route with the shortest prefix length.

57) Which two minimum parameters must be configured on an active interface to enable OSPFV2 to operate? (Choose two.)

A. OSPF process ID

B. OSPF MD5 authentication key

C. OSPF stub flag

D. IPv6 address

E. OSPF area

58)

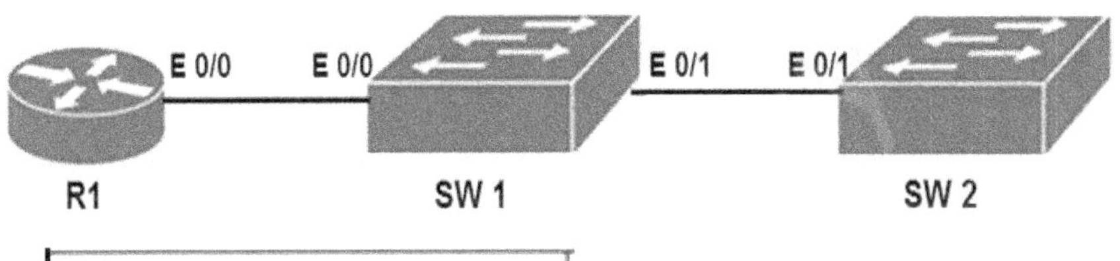

R1:

interface Ethernet0/0
  no ip address
!

SW1:

interface Ethernet0/0
  switchport trunk encapsulation dot1q
  switchport mode trunk
!
interface Ethernet0/1
  switchport trunk allowed vlan 10
  switchport trunk encapsulation dot1q
  switchport mode trunk

```
interface Ethernet0/1
  switchport trunk encapsulation dot1q
  switchport mode trunk
!
interface Ethernet0/2
  switchport access vlan 20
  switchport mode access
```

A. R1(config)#interface   ethernet0/0
R1(config)#encapsulation   dot1q   20
R1(config)#ip   address   10.20.20.1
255.255.255.0

B. R1(config)#interface   ethernet0/0.20
R1(config)#encapsulation   dot1q   20
R1(config)#ip   address   10.20.20.1
255.255.255.0

C. R1(config)#interface   ethernet0/0.20
R1(config)#ip   address   10.20.20.1
255.255.255.0

D. R1(config)#interface   ethernet0/0
R1(config)#ip   address   10.20.20.1
255.255.255.0

59)

```
R1#show ip interface brief
Interface                  IP-Address      OK?  Method
FastEthernet0/0            unassigned      YES  NVRAM
GigabitEthernet1/0         192.168.0.1     YES  NVRAM
GigabitEthernet2/0         10.10.1.10      YES  manual
GigabitEthernet3/0         10.10.10.20     YES  manual
GigabitEthernet4/0         unassigned      YES  NVRAM
Loopback0                  172.16.15.10    YES  manual

Status                  Protocol
administratively down   down
up                      up
up                      up
up                      up
administratively down   down
```

Refer to the exhibit. What does router R1 use as its OSPF router-ID?

A. 10.10.1.10

B. 10.10.10.20

C. 172.16.15.10

D. 192.168.0.1

60)

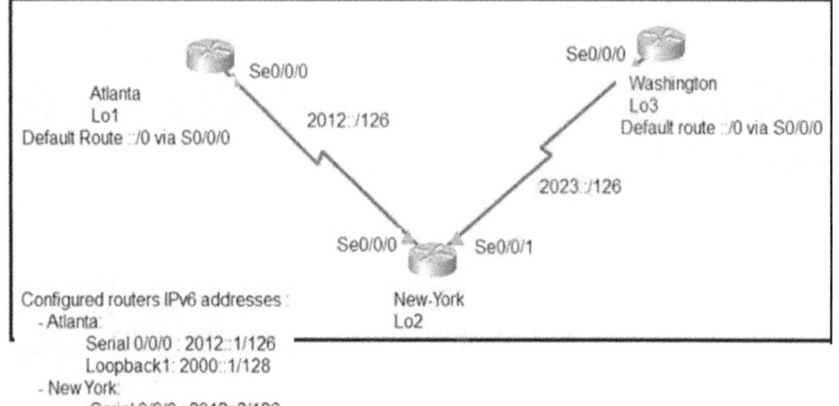

Refer to the exhibit. The loopback1 interface of the Atlanta router must reach the loopback3 interface of the Washington router.

Which two static host routes must be configured on the New York router? (Choose two.)

A. ipv6 route 2000::3/128 s0/0/0

B. ipv6 route 2000::1/128 s0/0/1

C. ipv6 route 2000::1/128 2012::1

D. ipv6 route 2000::1/128 2012::2

E. ipv6 route 2000::3/128 2023::3

61)

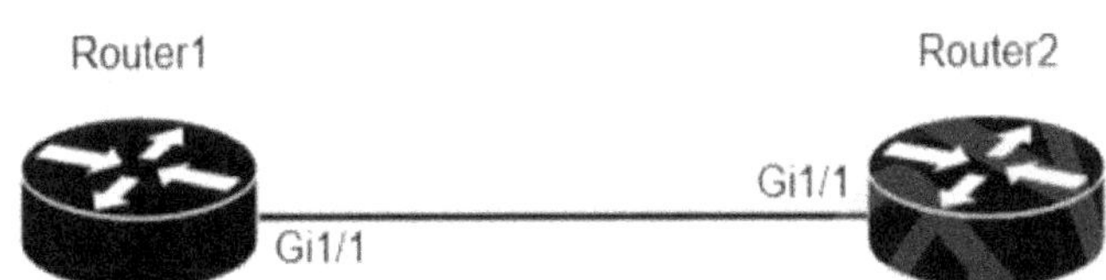


```
Router1(config)#interface GigabitEthernet1/1
Router1(config-if)#description ***Connection to Router2***
Router1(config-if)#ip address 10.10.10.1 255.255.255.252
Router1(config-if)#ip ospf hello-interval 5
Router1(config)#router ospf 1000
Router1(config-router)#router-id 1.1.1.1
Router1(config-router)#network 10.10.10.0 0.0.0.3 area 0

Router2(config)#interface GigabitEthernet1/1
Router2(config-if)#description ***Connection to Router1***
Router2(config-if)#ip address 10.10.10.2 255.255.255.252
Router2(config)#router ospf 1001
Router2(config-router)#router-id 2.2.2.2
Router2(config-router)#network 10.10.10.0 0.0.0.3 area 0
Router2(config-router)#passive-interface default
Router2(config-router)#no passive-interface GigabitEthernet1/1
```

Refer to the exhibit. After the configuration is applied, the two routers fail to establish an OSPF neighbor

relationship. What is the reason for the problem?

A. The OSPF process IDs are mismatched.

B. The network statement on Router1 is misconfigured.

C. Router2 is using the default hello timer.

D. The OSPF router IDs are mismatched.

62)

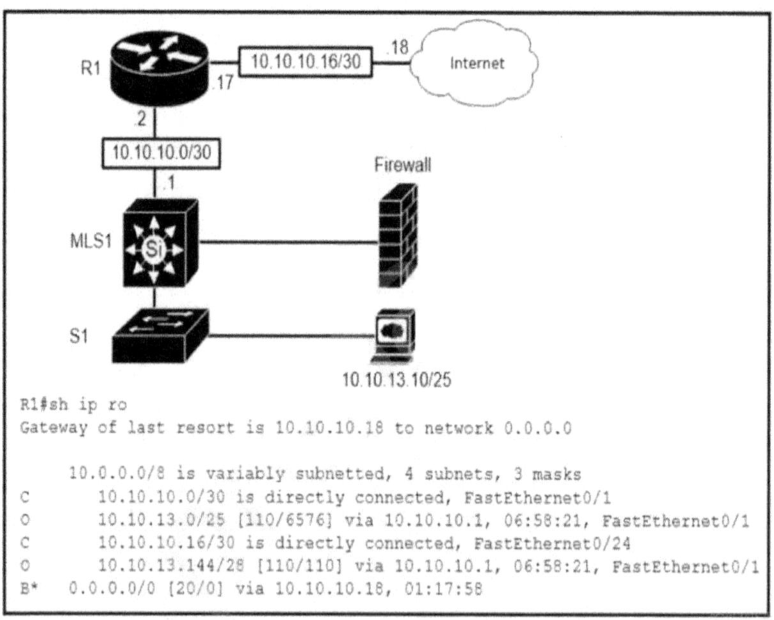


```
R1#sh ip ro
Gateway of last resort is 10.10.10.18 to network 0.0.0.0

     10.0.0.0/8 is variably subnetted, 4 subnets, 3 masks
C        10.10.10.0/30 is directly connected, FastEthernet0/1
O        10.10.13.0/25 [110/6576] via 10.10.10.1, 06:58:21, FastEthernet0/1
C        10.10.10.16/30 is directly connected, FastEthernet0/24
O        10.10.13.144/28 [110/110] via 10.10.10.1, 06:58:21, FastEthernet0/1
B*   0.0.0.0/0 [20/0] via 10.10.10.18, 01:17:58
```

Refer to the exhibit. Which route type is configured to reach the Internet?

A. floating static route.

B. host route.

C. network route.

D. default route.

63)

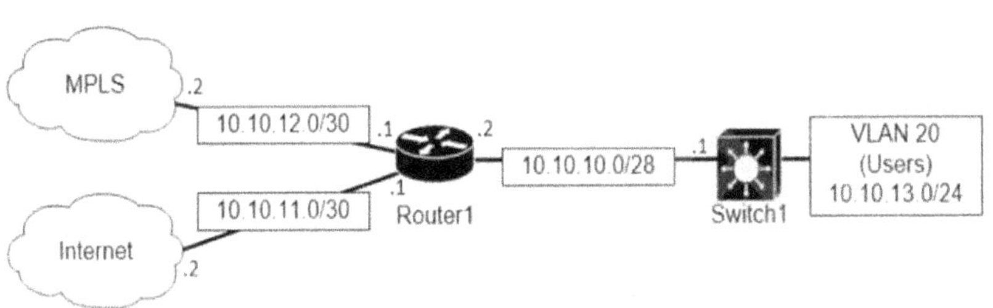


```
Router1#show ip route
Gateway of last resort is 10.10.11.2 to network 0.0.0.0
      209.165.200.0/27 is subnetted, 1 subnets
B        209.165.200.224 [20/0] via 10.10.12.2, 00:09:57
      10.0.0.0/8 is variably subnetted, 4 subnets, 3 masks
C        10.10.10.0/28 is directly connected, GigabitEthernet0/0
C        10.10.11.0/30 is directly connected, FastEthernet2/0
O        10.10.13.0/24 [110/2] via 10.10.10.1, 00:08:34, GigabitEthernet0/0
C        10.10.12.0/30 is directly connected, GigabitEthernet0/1
S*    0.0.0.0/0 [1/0] via 10.10.11.2

Switch1#show ip route
Gateway of last resort is not set
      10.0.0.0/8 is variably subnetted, 2 subnets, 2 masks
C        10.10.10.0/28 is directly connected, FastEthernet0/1
C        10.10.13.0/24 is directly connected, VLAN20
```

Refer to the exhibit. Which path is used by the router for Internet traffic?

A. 209.165.200.0/27

B. 0.0.0.0/0

C. 10.10.13.0/24

D. 10.10.10.0/28

64) When OSPF learns multiple paths to a network, how does it select a route?

A. For each existing interface, it adds the metric from the source router to the destination to calculate the route with the lowest bandwidth.

B. It counts the number of hops between the source router and the destination to determine the route with the lowest metric.

C. It divides a reference bandwidth of 100 Mbps by the actual bandwidth of the exiting interface to calculate the route with the lowest cost.

D. It multiplies the active K values by 256 to calculate the route with the lowest metric.

65) When a floating static route is configured, which action ensures that the backup route is used when the primary route fails?

A. The administrative distance must be higher on the primary route so that the backup route becomes secondary.

B. The default-information originate command must be configured for the route to be installed into the routing table.

C. The floating static route must have a lower administrative distance than the primary route so it is used as a backup.

D. The floating static route must have a higher administrative distance than the primary route so it is used as a backup.

66)

Designated Router (ID) 10.11.11.11, Interface address 10.10.10.1
Backup Designated router (ID) 10.3.3.3, Interface address 10.10.10.3
Timer intervals configured, Hello 10, Dead 40, Wait 40, Retransmit 5
oob-resync timeout 40
Hello due in 00:00:08
Supports Link-local Signaling (LLS)
Cisco NSF helper support enabled
IETF NSF helper support enabled
Index 1/1/1, flood queue length 0
Next 0x0(0)/0x0(0)/0x0(0)
Last flood scan length is 1. maximum is 6
Last flood scan time is 0 msec, maximum is 1 msec
Neighbor Count is 3, Adjacent neighbor count is 3
Adjacent with neighbor 10.1.1.4
Adjacent with neighbor 10.2.2.2
Adjacent with neighbor 10.3.3.3 (Backup Designated Router)
Suppress hello for 0 neighbor(s)

Refer to the exhibit. The show ip ospf interface command has been executed on R1. How is OSPF configured?

A. A point-to-point network type is configured.

B. The interface is not participating in OSPF.

C. The default Hello and Dead timers are in use.

D. There are six OSPF neighbors on this interface.

67) A user configured OSPF and advertised the Gigabit Ethernet interface in OSPF. By default, to which type of OSPF network does this interface belong?

A. point-to-multipoint.

B. point-to-point.

C. broadcast.

D. no broadcast.

68) Which attribute does a router use to select the best path when two or more different routes to the same destination exist from two different routing protocols?

A. dual algorithm.

B. metric.

C. administrative distance.

D. hop count.

69) Router A learns the same route from two different neighbors; one of the neighbor routers is an OSPF neighbor, and the other is an EIGRP neighbor.

What is the administrative distance of the route that will be installed in the routing table?

A. 20

B. 90

C. 110

D. 115

70)

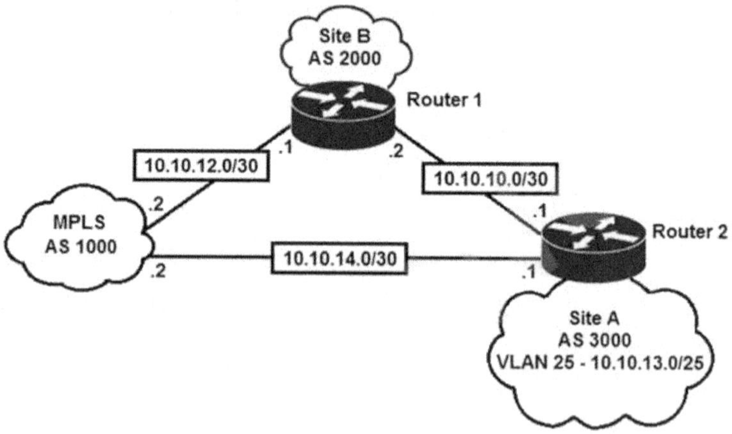

```
Router1#show ip route
Gateway of last resort is 10.10.11.2 to network 0.0.0.0
     10.0.0.0/8 is variably subnetted, 8 subnets, 4 masks
C        10.10.10.0/28 is directly connected, GigabitEthernet0/0
C        10.10.11.0/30 is directly connected, FastEthernet2/0
O        10.10.13.0/25 [110/2] via 10.10.10.1, 00:00:17, GigabitEthernet0/0
O        10.10.13.128/28 [110/2] via 10.10.10.1, 00:33:38, GigabitEthernet0/0
O        10.10.13.144/28 [110/2] via 10.10.10.1, 00:33:38, GigabitEthernet0/0
O        10.10.13.160/29 [110/2] via 10.10.10.1, 00:33:38, GigabitEthernet0/0
O        10.10.13.208/29 [110/2] via 10.10.10.1, 00:33:39, GigabitEthernet0/0
O        10.10.13.252/30 [110/2] via 10.10.10.1, 00:33:39, GigabitEthernet0/0
S*    0.0.0.0/0 [1/0] via 10.10.11.2
```

Refer to the exhibit. An engineer is bringing up a new circuit to the MPLS provider on the Gi0/1 interface of Router 1. The new circuit uses eBGP and learns the route to VLAN25 from the BGP path.

What is the expected behavior for the traffic flow for route 10.10.13.0/25?

A. Traffic to 10.10.13.0/25 is load balanced out of multiple interfaces.

B. Traffic to 10.10.13.0/25 is asymmetrical.

C. Route 10.10.13.0/25 is updated in the routing table as being learned from interface Gi0/1.

D. Route 10.10.13.0/25 learned via the Gi0/0 interface remains in the routing table.

71) Which two actions influence the EIGRP route selection process? (Choose two.)

A. The advertised distance is calculated by a downstream neighbor to inform the local router of the bandwidth on the link.

B. The router calculates the feasible distance of all paths to the destination route.

C. The router must use the advertised distance as the metric for any given route.

D. The router calculates the best backup path to the destination route and assigns it as the feasible successor.

E. The router calculates the reported distance by multiplying the delay on the exiting interface by 256.

72)

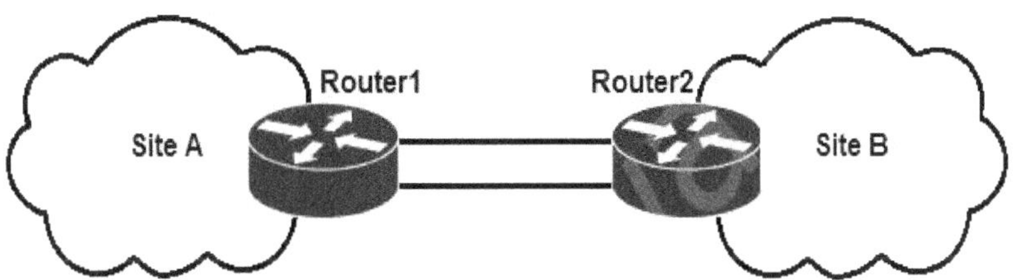


```
Roter2#show ip route
Gateway of last resort is not set

        10.0.0.0/8 is variably subnetted, 4 subnets, 2 masks
C           10.10.10.8/30 is directly connected, FastEthernet0/2
C           10.10.10.12/30 is directly connected, FastEthernet0/1
O           10.10.13.0/25 [110/11] via 10.10.10.9, 00:00:03, FastEthernet0/2
                          [110/11] via 10.10.10.13, 00:00:03, FastEthernet0/1
C           10.10.10.4/30 is directly connected, FastEthernet0/2
```

Refer to the exhibit. If OSPF is running on this network, how does Router2 handle traffic from Site B to 10.10.13.128/25 at Site A?

A. It sends packets out of interface Fa0/1 only.

B. It sends packets out of interface Fa0/2 only.

C. It load-balances traffic out of Fa0/1 and Fa0/2.

D. It cannot send packets to 10.10.13.128/25.

73) Which two outcomes are predictable behaviors for HSRP? (Choose two.)

A. The two routers negotiate one router as the active router and the other as the standby router.

B. The two routers share the same interface IP address, and default gateway traffic is load-balanced between them.

C. The two routers synchronize configurations to provide consistent packet forwarding.

D. Each router has a different IP address, both routers act as the default gateway on the LAN, and traffic is load-balanced between them.

E. The two routers share a virtual IP address that is used as the default gateway for devices on the LAN.

74)

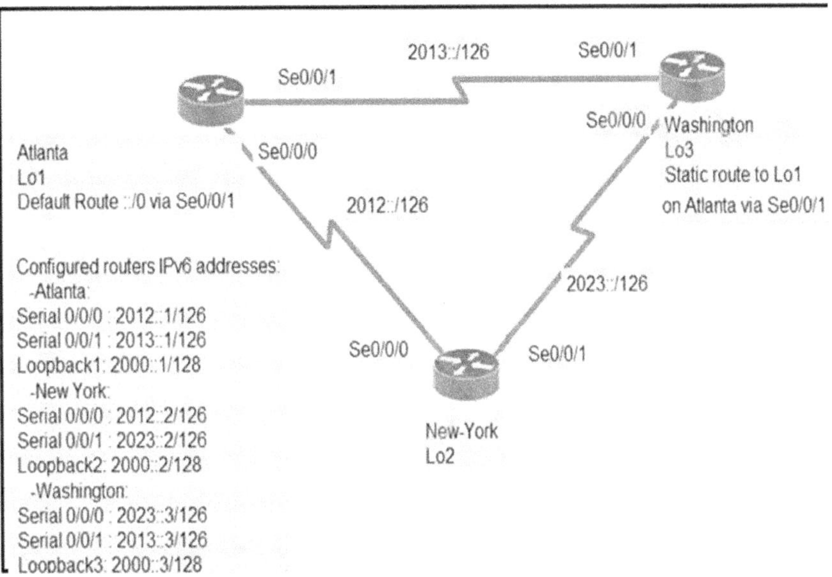

Refer to the exhibit. An engineer is configuring the New York router to reach the Lo1 interface of the Atlanta router using interface Se0/0/0 as the primary path.

Which two commands must be configured on the New York router so that it reaches the Lo1 interface of the Atlanta router via Washington when the link between New York and Atlanta goes down? (Choose two.)

A. Ipv6 route 2000::1/128 2012::1

B. Ipv6 route 2000::1/128 2012::1 5

C. Ipv6 route 2000::1/128 2012::2

D. Ipv6 route 2000::1/128 2023::2 5

E. Ipv6 route 2000::1/128 2023::3 5

75) How does HSRP provide first hop redundancy?

A. It load-balances Layer 2 traffic along the path by flooding traffic out all interfaces configured with the same VLAN.

B. It uses a shared virtual MAC and a virtual IP address to a group of routers that serve as the default gateway for hosts on a LAN.

C. It forwards multiple packets to the same destination over different routed links in the data path.

D. It load-balances traffic by assigning the same metric value to more than one route to the same destination in the IP routing table.

76) Refer to the exhibit. Which action establishes the OSPF neighbor relationship without forming an adjacency?

```
R1# sh ip ospf int gig0/0
Gig0/0 is up, line protocol is up
        Internet Address 10.201.24.8/28, Area 1, Attached via Network Statement
        Process ID 100, Router ID 192.168.1.1, Network Type BROADCAST, Cost: 1
        Topology-MTID        Cost           Disabled        Shutdown       Topology Name
              0               1                no              no             Base
        Transmit Delay is 1 sec, State DR, Priority 1
        Designated Router (ID) 192.168.1.1, Interface address 10.201.24.8
        No backup designated router on this network
        Timer intervals configured, Hello 10, Dead 40, Wait 40, Retransmit 5
            oob-resync timeout 40
            Hello due in 00:00:07

R2#sh ip ospf int gig0/0
gig0/0 is up, line protocol is up
        Internet Address 10.201.24.1/28, Area 1
        Process ID 100, Router ID 172.16.1.1, Network Type BROADCAST, Cost: 1
        Transmit Delay is 1 sec, State DR, Priority 1
        Designated Router (ID) 172.16.1.1, Interface address 10.201.24.1
        No backup designated router on this network
        Timer intervals configured, Hello 20, Dead 80, Wait 80, Retransmit 5
```

A. modify hello interval.

B. modify process ID.

C. modify priority.

D. modify network type.

77) Which command must you enter to guarantee that an HSRP router with higher priority becomes the HSRP primary router after it is reloaded?

A. standby 10 preempt

B. standby 10 version 1

C. standby 10 priority 150

D. standby 10 version 2

78) Which command should you enter to verify the priority of a router in an HSRP group?

A. show hsrp.

B. show sessions.

C. show interfaces.

D. show standby.

79) Refer to the exhibit.

Which command would you use to configure a static route on Router1 to network 192.168.202.0/24 with a nondefault administrative distance?

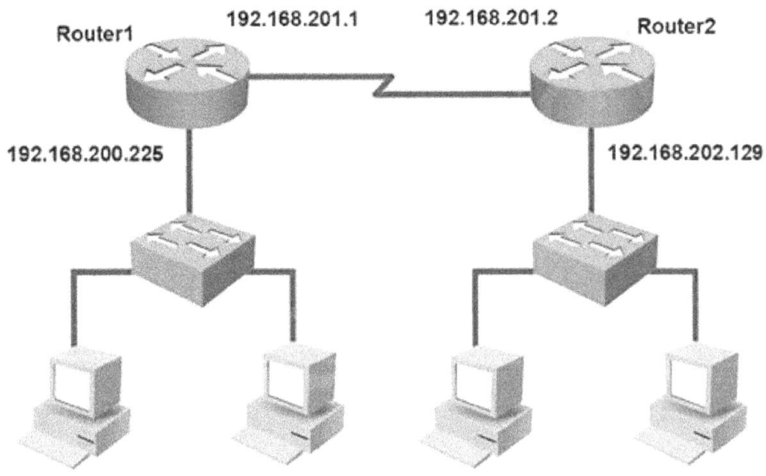

A. router1(config)#ip route 192.168.202.0 255.255.255.0 192.168.201.2 1

B. router1(config)#ip route 192.168.202.0 255.255.255.0 192.168.201.2 5

C. router1(config)#ip route 1 192.168.201.1 255.255.255.0 192.168.201.2

D. router1(config)#ip route 5 192.168.202.0 255.255.255.0 192.168.201.2

80) Which of the following dynamic routing protocols are Distance Vector routing protocols? (CHOOSE 2)

A. IS-IS

B. EIGRP

C. OSPF

D. BGP

E. RIP

81) You have configured a router with an OSPF router ID, but its IP address still reflects the physical interface.

Which action can you take to correct the problem in the least disruptive way?

A. Reload the OSPF process.

B. Specify a loopback address.

C. Reboot the router.

D. Save the router configuration.

82) Which command should you enter to view the error log in an EIGRP for IPv6 environment?

A. show ipv6 eigrp neighbors.

B. show ipv6 eigrp topology.

C. show ipv6 eigrp traffic.

D. show ipv6 eigrp events.

83) Refer to the exhibit. Which two statements about the network

environment of router R1 must be true? (Choose two.)

```
R1#show ip route
Gateway of last resort is 10.85.33.14 to network 0.0.0.0
D*EX  0.0.0.0/0
          [170/257024] via 10.85.33.14, 7w0d, TenGigabitEthernet0/2/0.100
          [170/257024] via 10.85.33.10, 7w0d, TenGigabitEthernet0/1/0.100
      10.0.0.0/8 is variably subnetted, 6692 subnets, 20 masks
B         10.0.0.0/8 [20/0] via 10.48.144.14, 1w5d
D EX      10.0.1.0/24
          [170/51968] via 10.85.33.14, 7w0d, TenGigabitEthernet0/2/0.100
          [170/51968] via 10.85.33.10, 7w0d, TenGigabitEthernet0/1/0.100
D EX      10.0.2.0/23
          [170/51968] via 10.85.33.14, 7w0d, TenGigabitEthernet0/2/0.100
          [170/51968] via 10.85.33.10, 7w0d, TenGigabitEthernet0/1/0.100
D EX      10.0.4.0/22
          [170/51968] via 10.85.33.14, 7w0d, TenGigabitEthernet0/2/0.100
          [170/51968] via 10.85.33.10, 7w0d, TenGigabitEthernet0/1/0.100
D EX      10.0.8.0/21
          [170/51968] via 10.85.33.14, 7w0d, TenGigabitEthernet0/2/0.100
          [170/51968] via 10.85.33.10, 7w0d, TenGigabitEthernet0/1/0.100
D EX      10.0.16.0/20
          [170/51968] via 10.85.33.14, 7w0d, TenGigabitEthernet0/2/0.100
          [170/51968] via 10.85.33.10, 7w0d, TenGigabitEthernet0/1/0.100
D EX      10.0.32.0/19
          [170/51968] via 10.85.33.14, 7w0d, TenGigabitEthernet0/2/0.100
          [170/51968] via 10.85.33.10, 7w0d, TenGigabitEthernet0/1/0.100
B         10.1.96.0/23 [20/0] via 10.111.33.217, 2w3d
B         10.1.96.0/24 [20/0] via 10.111.33.217, 2w3d
B         10.1.97.0/24 [20/0] via 10.111.33.217, 4w5d
D EX      10.1.255.240/28
          [170/51968] via 10.85.33.14, 7w0d, TenGigabitEthernet0/2/0.100
          [170/51968] via 10.85.33.10, 7w0d, TenGigabitEthernet0/1/0.100
D EX      10.2.0.0/16
          [170/51968] via 10.85.33.14, 7w0d, TenGigabitEthernet0/2/0.100
          [170/51968] via 10.85.33.10, 7w0d, TenGigabitEthernet0/1/0.100
B         10.2.0.0/24 [20/0] via 10.111.33.217, 4w5d
B         10.2.96.0/23 [20/0] via 10.48.144.14, 4w5d
B         10.2.96.0/24 [20/0] via 10.48.144.14, 3w1d
B         10.2.97.0/24 [20/0] via 10.48.144.14, 4w5d
D EX      10.3.0.0/16
          [170/51968] via 10.85.33.14, 7w0d, TenGigabitEthernet0/2/0.100
          [170/51968] via 10.85.33.10, 7w0d, TenGigabitEthernet0/1/0.100
B         10.5.1.0/24 [20/0] via 10.111.33.217, 1w4d
B         10.5.5.0/24 [20/0] via 10.111.33.217, 4w3d
B         10.6.0.0/24 [20/0] via 10.111.33.217, 3w3d
```

A. The EIGRP administrative distance was manually changed from 90 to 170.

B. There are 20 different network masks within the 10.0.0.0/8 network.

C. Ten routes are equally load-balanced between Te0/1/0.100 and Te0/2/0.100.

D. The 10.0.0.0/8 network was learned via external EIGRP.

E. A static default route to 10.85.33.14 was defined.

84) Which two statements about exterior routing protocols are true? (Choose two.)

A. They determine the optimal within an autonomous system.

B. They determine the optimal path between autonomous systems.

C. BGP is the current standard exterior routing protocol.

D. Most modern networking supports both EGP and BGP for external routing.

E. Most modern network routers support both EGP and EIGRP for external routing.

85) You have two paths for the 10.10.10.0 network - one that has a feasible distance of 3072 and the other of 6144.

What do you need to do to load balance your EIGRP routes? (CHOOSE 2)

A. Change the maximum paths to 2.

B. Change the configuration so they both have the same feasible distance.

C. Change the variance for the path that has a feasible distance of 3072 to 2.

D. Change the IP addresses so both paths have the same source IP address.

86) Which two circumstances can prevent two routers from establishing an OSPF neighbor adjacency? (Choose two.)

A. mismatched autonomous system numbers.

B. an ACL blocking traffic from multicast address 224.0.0.10.

C. mismatched process IDs.

D. mismatched hello timers and dead timers.

E. use of the same router ID on both devices.

87) Which three describe the reasons large OSPF networks use a hierarchical design? (Choose three.)

A. to speed up convergence.

B. to reduce routing overhead.

C. to lower costs by replacing routers with distribution layer switches.

D. to decrease latency by increasing bandwidth.

E. to confine network instability to single areas of the network.

F. to reduce the complexity of router configuration.

88) Refer to the exhibit. If R1 receives a packet destined to 172.16.1.1, to which IP address does it send the packet?

```
R1@show ip route
Codes:  C - connected, S - static, R - RIP, M - mobile, B - BGP
        D - EIGRP, EX - EIGRP external, O - OSPF, IA - OSPF inter area
        N1 - OSPF NSSA external type 1, N2 - OSPF NSSA external type 2
        E1 - OSPF external type 1, E2 - OSPF external type 2
        i - IS-IS, su - IS-IS summary, L1 - IS-IS level-1, L2 - IS-IS level-2
        ia - IS-IS inter area, * - candidate default, U - per-user static route
        o - ODR, P - periodic downloaded static route

Gateway of last resort is 192.168.14.4 to network 0.0.0.0

C    192.168.12.0/24 is directly connected, FastEthernet0/0
C    192.168.13.0/24 is directly connected, FastEthernet0/1
C    192.168.14.0/24 is directly connected, FastEthernet1/0
     192.168.10.0/24 is variably subnetted, 3 subnets, 3 masks
O       192.168.10.0/24 [110/2] via 192.168.14.4, 00:02:01, FastEthernet1/0
O       192.168.10.32/27 [110/11] via 192.168.13.3, 00:00:52, FastEthernet0/1
O       192.168.0.0/16 [110/2] via 192.168.15.5, 00:05:01, FastEthernet1/1
D       192.168.10.1/32 [90/52778] via 192.168.12.2, 00:03:44, FastEthernet0/0
O*E2 0.0.0.0/0 [110/1] via 192.168.14.4, 00:00:10, FastEthernet1/0
```

A. 192.168.14.4

B. 192.168.12.2

C. 192.168.13.3

D. 192.168.15.5

89) Refer to the exhibit. On R1 which routing protocol is in use on the route to 192.168.10.1?

```
R1#show ip route
Codes: C - connected, S - static, R - RIP, M - mobile, B - BGP
       D - EIGRP, EX - EIGRP external, O - OSPF, IA - OSPF inter area
       N1 - OSPF NSSA external type 1, N2 - OSPF NSSA external type 2
       E1 - OSPF external type 1, E2 - OSPF external type 2
       i - IS-IS, su - IS-IS summary, L1 - IS-IS level-1, L2 - IS-IS level-2
       ia - IS-IS inter area, * - candidate default, U - per-user static route
       o - ODR, P - periodic downloaded static route

Gateway of last resort is 192.168.14.4 to network 0.0.0.0

C    192.168.12.0/24 is directly connected, FastEthernet0/0
C    192.168.13.0/24 is directly connected, FastEthernet0/1
C    192.168.14.0/24 is directly connected, FastEthernet1/0
     192.168.10.0/24 is variably subnetted, 3 subnets, 3 masks
O       192.168.10.0/24 [110/2] via 192.168.14.4, 00:02:01, FastEthernet1/0
O       192.168.10.32/27 [110/11] via 192.168.13.3, 00:00:52, FastEthernet0/1
O       192.168.0.0/16 [110/2] via 192.168.15.5, 00:05:01, FastEthernet1/1
D       192.168.10.1/32 [90/52778] via 192.168.12.2, 00:03:44, FastEthernet0/0
O*E2 0.0.0.0/0 [110/1] via 192.168.14.4, 00:00:10, FastEthernet1/0
```

A. RIP

B. OSPF

C. IGRP

D. EIGRP

90) Refer to the exhibit. Which Command do you enter so that R1 advertises the loopback0 interface to the BGP Peers?

```
R1
interface Loopback0
    ip address 172.16.1.33 255.255.255.224

interface FastEthernet0/0
    ip address 192.168.12.1 255.255.255.0

router bgp 100
neighbor 192.168.12.2 remote-as 100
```

A. Network 172.16.1.32 mask 255.255.255.224

B. Network 172.16.1.0 0.0.0.255

C. Network 172.16.1.32 255.255.255.224

D. Network 172.16.1.33 mask 255.255.255.224

E. Network 172.16.1.32 mask 0.0.0.31

F. Network 172.16.1.32 0.0.0.31

91) Refer to exhibit.

What Administrative distance has route to 192.168.10.1?

```
R1@show ip route
Codes: C - connected, S - static, R - RIP, M - mobile, B - BGP
       D - EIGRP, EX - EIGRP external, O - OSPF, IA - OSPF inter area
       N1 - OSPF NSSA external type 1, N2 - OSPF NSSA external type 2
       E1 - OSPF external type 1, E2 - OSPF external type 2
       i - IS-IS, su - IS-IS summary, L1 - IS-IS level-1, L2 - IS-IS level-2
       ia - IS-IS inter area, * - candidate default, U - per-user static route
       o - ODR, P - periodic downloaded static route

Gateway of last resort is 192.168.14.4 to network 0.0.0.0

C    192.168.12.0/24 is directly connected, FastEthernet0/0
C    192.168.13.0/24 is directly connected, FastEthernet0/1
C    192.168.14.0/24 is directly connected, FastEthernet1/0
     192.168.10.0/24 is variably subnetted, 3 subnets, 3 masks
O       192.168.10.0/24 [110/2] via 192.168.14.4, 00:02:01, FastEthernet1/0
O       192.168.10.32/27 [110/11] via 192.168.13.3, 00:00:52, FastEthernet0/1
O       192.168.0.0/16 [110/2] via 192.168.15.5, 00:05:01, FastEthernet1/1
D       192.168.10.1/32 [90/52778] via 192.168.12.2, 00:03:44, FastEthernet0/0
O*E2 0.0.0.0/0 [110/1] via 192.168.14.4, 00:00:10, FastEthernet1/0
```

A. 1

B. 90

C. 110

D. 120

92) Which value is used to determine the active router in an HSRP default configuration?

A. Router loopback address.

B. Router IP address.

C. Router priority.

D. Router tracking number.

93) Refer to the exhibit. If RTR01 is configured as shown, which three addresses will be received by other routers that are running EIGRP on the network? (Choose three.)

```
RTR01 (config) #router eigrp 103
RTR01 (config-router) #network 10.4.3.0
RTR01 (config-router) #network 172.16.4.0
RTR01 (config-router) #network 192.168.2.0
RTR01 (config-router) #auto-summary
```

A. 192.168.2.0

B. 10.4.3.0

C. 10.0.0.0

D. 172.16.0.0

E. 172.16.4.0

F. 192.168.0.0

94) Which configuration command can you apply to a HSRP router so that its local interface becomes active if all other routers in the group fail?

A. no additional config is required

B. standby 1 track ethernet

C. standby 1 preempt

D. standby 1 priority 250

95) Which two statements about eBGP neighbor relationships are true? (Choose two.)

A. The two devices must reside in different autonomous systems.

B. Neighbors must be specifically declared in the configuration of each device.

C. They can be created dynamically after the network statement is configured.

D. The two devices must reside in the same autonomous system.

E. The two devices must have matching timer settings.

96) Refer to the exhibit. How will the router handle a packet destined for 192.0.2.156?

```
router#show ip route
     Codes: C - connected, S - static, I - IGRP, R - RIP, M - mobile, B - BGP, D - EIGRP
     EX - EIGRP external, O - OSPF, IA - OSPF inter area, N1 - OSPF NSSA external type 1,
     N2 - OSPF NSSA external type 2, E1 - OSPF external type 1, E2 - OSPF external type 2,
     E - EGP, i - IS-IS, L1 - IS-IS level-1, L2 - IS-IS level-2. * - candidate default, U - per-user
     static route, o - ODR

Gateway of last resort is 192.168.4.1 to network 0.0.0.0

     10.0.0.0/24 is subnetted, 3 subnets
C          10.0.2.0 is directly connected, Ethernet1
D          10.0.3.0 [90/2195456] via 192.168.1.2, 00:03:01, Serial0
D          10.0.4.0 [90/2195456] via 192.168.3.1, 00:03:01, Serial1
C       192.168.1.0/24 is directly connected, Serial0
D       192.168.2.0/24 [90/2681856] via 192.168.1.2, 00:03:01, Serial0
                       [90/2681856] via 192.168.3.1, 00:03:01, Serial1
C       192.168.3.0/24 is directly connected, Serial1
C       192.168.4.0/24 is directly connected, Serial2
```

A. The router will forward the packet via either Serial0 or Serial1.

B. The router will return the packet to its source.

C. The router will forward the packet via Serial2.

D. The router will drop the packet.

97) Which statements describe the routing protocol OSPF? (Choose three.)

A. It supports VLSM.

B. It is used to route between autonomous systems.

C. It confines network instability to one area of the network.

D. It increases routing overhead on the network.

E. It allows extensive control of routing updates.

F. It is simpler to configure than RIP v2.

98) Refer to the exhibit. After you apply the given configurations to R1 and R2 you notice that OSPFv3 fails to start.

```
R1
ipv6 unicast-routing

interface FastEthernet0/0
    no ip address
ipv6 enable
    ipv6 address 3001:DBB:13::1/64
    ipv6 ospf 1 area 0
ipv6 router ospf 1
router-id 172.16.1.1

R2
ipv6 unicast-routing

interface FastEthernet0/0
    no ip address
    ipv6 enable
    ipv6 address 2001:DBB:12::12/64
    ipv6 ospf 1 area 3
ipv6 router ospf 1
router-id 172.16.3.3
```

A. The area numbers on R1 and R2 are mismatched.

B. The IPv6 network addresses on R1 and R2 are mismatched.

C. The autonomous system numbers on R1 and R2 are mismatched.

D. The router ids on R1 and R2 are mismatched.

99) Which command is used to display the collection of OSPF link states?

A. show ip ospf link-state.

B. show ip ospf lsa database.

C. show ip ospf neighbors.

D. show ip ospf database.

100) Refer to the exhibit. A network associate has configured OSPF with the command:

City(config-router)   #   network 192.168.12.64 0.0.0.63 area 0

After completing the configuration, the associate discovers that not all the interfaces are participating in OSPF. Which

three of the interfaces shown in the exhibit will participate in OSPF according to this configuration statement? (Choose three.)

```
City#show ip interface brief

Interface            IP-Address        OK?    Method    Status   Protocol
FastEthernet0/0      192.168.12.48     Yes    manual    up       up
FastEthernet0/1      192.168.12.65     Yes    manual    up       up
Serial0/0            192.168.12.121    Yes    manual    up       up
Seriak0/1            unassigned        Yes    unset     up       up
Serial0/1.102        192.168.12.125    Yes    manual    up       up
Serial0/1.103        192.168.12.129    Yes    manual    up       up
Serial0/1.104        192.168.12.133    Yes    manual    up       up
City#
```

A. FastEthernet0 /0

B. FastEthernet0 /1

C. Serial0/0

D. Serial0/1.102

E. Serial0/1.103

F. Serial0/1.104

101) Refer to the exhibit. C-router is to be used as a "router-on-a-stick" to route between the VLANs. All the interfaces have

been properly configured and IP routing is operational. The hosts in the VLANs have been configured with the appropriate default gateway. What is true about this configuration?

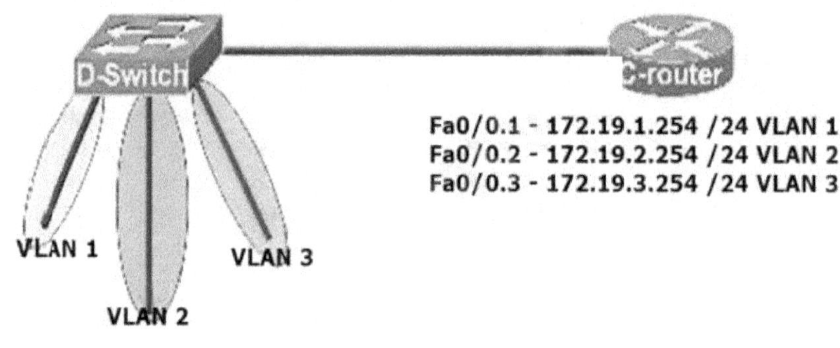

A. These commands need to be added to the configuration: C-router(config)# router eigrp 123 C-router(config-router)# network 172.19.0.0

B. These commands need to be added to the configuration: C-router(config)# router ospf 1 C-router(config-router)# network 172.19.0.0 0.0.3.255 area 0

C. These commands need to be added to the configuration: C-router(config)# router rip C-router(config-router)# network 172.19.0.0

D. No further routing configuration is required.

102) Refer to the exhibit. Which address and mask combination represents a summary of the routes learned by EIGRP?

Gateway of last resort is not set

     192.168.25.0/30 is subnetted, 4 subnets
D   192.168.25.20 [90/2681856] via 192.168.15.5, 00:00:10, Serial0/1
D   192.168.25.16 [90/1823638] via 192.168.15.5, 00:00:50, Serial0/1
D   192.168.25.24 [90/3837233] via 192.168.15.5, 00:05:23, Serial0/1
D   192.168.25.28 [90/8127323] via 192.168.15.5, 00:06:45, Serial0/1
C   192.168.15.4/30 is directly connected, Serial0/1
C   192.168.2.0/24 is directly connected, FastEthernet0/0

A. 192.168.25.0 255.255.255.240

B. 192.168.25.0 255.255.255.252

C. 192.168.25.16 255.255.255.240

D. 192.168.25.16 255.255.255.252

E. 192.168.25.28 255.255.255.240

F. 192.168.25.28 255.255.255.252

103) Refer to the exhibit.

Given the output for this command, if the router ID has not been manually set, what router ID will OSPF use for this router?

```
RouterD#    show ip interface brief
Interface          IP-Address      OK?    Method Status Protocol
FastEthernet0/0    192.168.5.3     Yes    manual    up       up
FastEthernet0/1    10.1.1.2        Yes    manual    up       up
Loopback0          172.16.5.1      Yes    NVRAM     up       up
Loopback1          10.154.154.1    Yes    NVRAM     up       up
```

A. 10.1.1.2

B. 10.154.154.1

C. 172.16.5.1

D. 192.168.5.3

104) Refer to the exhibit.

When running EIGRP, what is required for RouterA to exchange routing updates with RouterC?

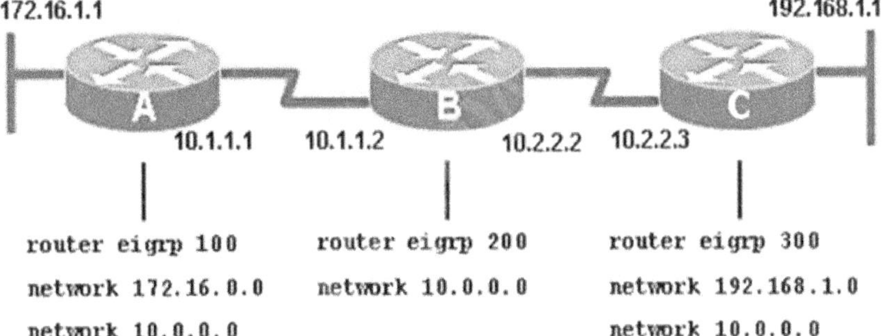

A. AS numbers must be changed to match on all the routers.

B. Loopback interfaces must be configured so a DR is elected.

C. The no auto-summary command is needed on Router A and Router C.

D. Router B needs to have two network statements, one for each connected network.

105) A network administrator is troubleshooting the OSPF configuration of routers R1 and R2. The routers cannot

establish an adjacency relationship on their common Ethernet link.

R1: Ethernet0 is up, line protocol is up
Internet address 192.168.1.2/24, Area 0
Process ID 1, Router ID 192.168.31.33, Network Type BROADCAST, Cost: 10
Transmit Delay is 1 sec, State DR, Priority 1
Designated Router (ID) 192.168.31.33, Interface address 192.168.1.2
No backup designated router on this network
Timer intervals configured, Hello 5. Dead 20, Wait 20, Retransmit 5

R2: Ethernet0 is up, line protocol is up
Internet address 192.168.1.2/24, Area 0
Process ID 2, Router ID 192.168.31.11, Network Type BROADCAST, Cost: 10
Transmit Delay is 1 sec, State DR, Priority 1
Designated Router (ID) 192.168.31.11, Interface address 192.168.1.1
No backup designated router on this network
Timer intervals configured, Hello 10, Dead 40, Wait 40, Retransmit 5

The graphic shows the output of the show ip ospf interface e0 command for routers R1 and R2. Based on the information in the graphic, what is the cause of this problem?

A. The OSPF area is not configured properly.

B. The priority on R1 should be set higher.

C. The cost on R1 should be set higher.

D. The hello and dead timers are not configured properly.

E. A backup designated router needs to be added to the network.

F. The OSPF process ID numbers must match.

106) Refer to the exhibit. Which two statements are true about the loopback address that is configured on RouterB? (Choose two.)

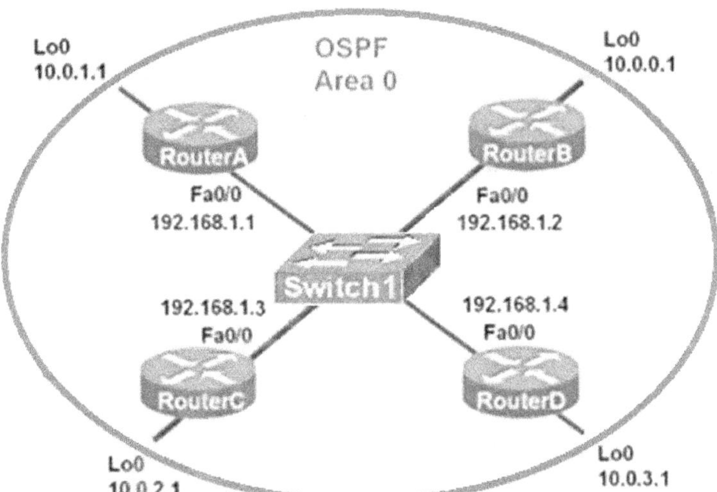

A. It ensures that data will be forwarded by RouterB.

B. It provides stability for the OSPF process on RouterB.

C. It specifies that the router ID for RouterB should be 10.0.0.1.

D. It decreases the metric for routes that are advertised from RouterB.

E. It indicates that RouterB should be elected the DR for the LAN.

107) If all OSPF routers in a single area are configured with the same priority value, what value does a router use for the OSPF router ID in the absence of a loopback interface?

A. the IP address of the first Fast Ethernet interface.

B. the IP address of the console management interface.

C. the highest IP address among its active interfaces.

D. the lowest IP address among its active interfaces.

E. the priority value until a loopback interface is configured.

108) The OSPF Hello protocol performs which of the following tasks? (Choose two.)

A. It provides dynamic neighbor discovery.

B. It detects unreachable neighbors in 90 second intervals.

C. It maintains neighbor relationships.

D. It negotiates correctness parameters between neighboring interfaces.

E. It uses timers to elect the router with the fastest links as the designated router.

F. It broadcasts hello packets throughout the internetwork to discover all routers that are running OSPF.

109) What are two requirements for an HSRP group? (Choose two.)

A. exactly one active router.

B. one or more standby routers.

C. one or more backup virtual routers.

D. exactly one standby active router.

E. exactly one backup virtual router.

110) Which two pieces of information can you learn by viewing the routing table? (Choose two.)

A. whether an ACL was applied inbound or outbound to an interface.

B. the EIGRP or BGP autonomous system.

C. whether the administrative distance was manually or dynamically configured.

D. which neighbor adjacencies are established.

E. the length of time that a route has been known.

111)

```
       10.0.0.0/24 is subsetted, 1 subnets
C         10.0.0.0 is directly connected, FastEthernet0/1
C      172.160.0/16 is directly connected, FastEthernet0/0
D      192.168.0.0/24 [90/30720] via 172.16.0.2, 00:00:03, FastEthernet0/0
```

Refer to the exhibit. Which route type does the routing protocol Code D represent in the output?

A. statically assigned route.

B. route learned through EIGRP.

C. /24 route of a locally configured IP.

D. internal BGP route.

112) An engineer must configure an OSPF neighbor relationship between router R1 and R3. The authentication configuration has been configured and the connecting interfaces are in the same 192.168.1.0/30

subnet. What are the next two steps to complete the configuration? (Choose two.)

A. configure the interfaces as OSPF active on both sides.

B. configure both interfaces with the same area ID.

C. configure the hello and dead timers to match on both sides.

D. configure the same process ID for the router OSPF process.

E. configure the same router ID on both routing processes.

113)

```
R1# show ip route | begin gateway
Gateway of last resort is 209.165.200.246 to network 0.0.0.0
S* 0.0.0.0/0 [1/0] via 209.165.200.246, Serial0/1/0
      is directly connected, Serial0/1/0
      172.16.0.0/16 is variably subnetted, 2 subnets, 2 masks
S     172.16.3.0/24 [1/0] via 209.165.200.250, Serial0/0/0
O     172.16.3.0/28 [110/1] via 209.165.200.254, 00:00:28, Serial0/0/1
      209.165.200.0/24 is variably subnetted, 6 subnets, 2 masks
C     209.165.200.244/30 is directly connected, Serial0/1/0
L     209.165.200.245/32 is directly connected, Serial0/1/0
C     209.165.200.248/30 is directly connected, Serial0/0/0
L     209.165.200.249/32 is directly connected, Serial0/0/0
C     209.165.200.252/30 is directly connected, Serial0/0/1
L     209.165.200.253/32 is directly connected, Serial0/0/1
```

Refer to the exhibit. A packet is being sent across router R1 to host 172.16.0.14. What is the destination route for the packet?

A. 209.165.200.250 via Serial0/0/0

B. 209.165.200.254 via Serial0/0/0

C. 209.165.200.254 via Serial0/0/1

D. 209.165.200.246 via Serial0/1/0

114)

```
R1# show ip route | begin gateway
Gateway of last resort is 209.165.200.246 to network 0.0.0.0
S* 0.0.0.0/0 [1/0] via 209.165.200.246, Serial0/1/0
      is directly connected, Serial0/1/0
      172.16.0.0/16 is variably subnetted, 2 subnets, 2 masks
S      172.16.3.0/24 [1/0] via 207.165.200.250, Serial0/0/0
O      172.16.3.0/28 [110/84437] via 207.165.200.254, 00:00:28, Serial0/0/1
      207.165.200.0/24 is variably subnetted, 6 subnets, 2 masks
C      207.165.200.244/30 is directly connected, Serial0/1/0
L      207.165.200.245/32 is directly connected, Serial0/1/0
C      207.165.200.248/30 is directly connected, Serial0/0/0
L      207.165.200.249/32 is directly connected, Serial0/0/0
C      207.165.200.252/30 is directly connected, Serial0/0/1
L      207.165.200.253/32 is directly connected, Serial0/0/1
```

Refer to the exhibit. A packet is being sent across router R1 to host 172.16.3.14. To which destination does the router send the packet?

A. 207.165.200.246 via Serial0/1/0

B. 207.165.200.254 via Serial0/0/0

C. 207.165.200.250 via Serial0/0/0

D. 207.165.200.254 via Serial0/0/1

115)

```
R1#config t
R1(config)# interface gi1/1
R1(config-if)# ip address 192.168.0.1 255.255.255.0

R1(config)# router bgp 65000
R1(config-router)# neighbor 192.168.0.2 remote-as 65001
R1(config-router)# network 10.1.1.0 mask 255.255.255.0

R1(config)# router ospf 1
R1(config)# router-id 1.1.1.1
R1(config)# network 192.168.0.1 0.0.0.0 area 0
R1(config)# network 10.1.1.0 0.0.0.255 area 0

R1(config)# router eigrp 1
R1(config)# eigrp router-id 1.1.1.1
R1(config)# network 10.1.1.0 0.0.0.255
R1(config)# network 192.168.0.1 0.0.0.0

R2#config t
R2(config)# interface gi1/1
R2(config-if)# ip address 192.168.0.2 255.255.255.0

R2#config t
R2(config)# router bgp 65001
R2(config-router)# neighbor 192.168.0.1 remote-as 65000

R2(config)# router ospf 1
R2(config)# router-id 2.2.2.2
R2(config)# network 192.168.1.2 0.0.0.0 area 0

R2(config)# router eigrp 1
R2(config)# eigrp router-id 1.1.1.1
R2(config)# network 192.168.0.1 0.0.0.0

R2(config)# ip route 10.1.1.0 255.255.255.0 192.168.0.1
```

Refer to the exhibit. Router R2 is configured with multiple routes to reach network 10.1.1.0/24 from router R1. Which path is chosen by router R2 to reach the destination network 10.1.1.0/24?

A. static

B. EIGRP

C. eBGP

D. OSPF

116)

```
R1# show ip route
Codes:   C - connected, S - static, I - IGRP, R - RIP, M - mobile, B - BGP
         D - EIGRP, EX - EIGRP external, O - OSPF, IA - OSPF inter area
         N1 - OSPF NSSA external type 1, N2 - OSPF NSSA external type 2
         E1 - OSPF external type 1, E2 - OSPF external type 2, E - EGP
         i - IS-IS, L1 - IS-IS level-1, L2 - IS-IS level-2, * - candidate default
         U - per-user static route, o - ODR
Gateway of last resort is not set
C        1.0.0.0/8 is directly connected, Loopback0
         10.0.0.0/8 is variably subnetted, 4 subnets, 2 masks
O            10.0.1.3/32 [110/100] via 10.0.1.3, 00:39:08, Serial0
C            10.0.1.0/24 is directly connected, Serial0
O            10.0.1.5/32 [110/5] via 10.0.1.50, 00:39:08, Serial0
O            10.0.1.4/32 [110/10] via 10.0.1.4, 00:39:08, Serial0
```

Refer to the exhibit. What is the next hop address for traffic that is destined to host 10.0.1.5?

A. Loopback 0

B. 10.0.1.4

C. 10.0.1.3

D. 10.0.1.50

117)

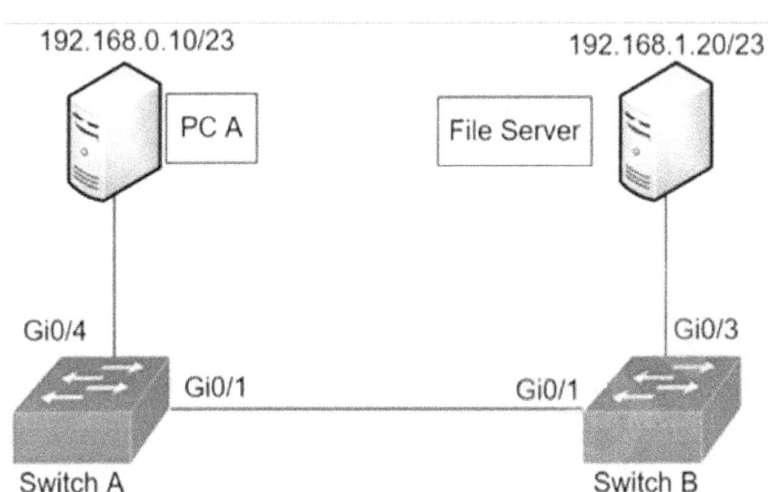

Switch A
Vlan 10,11,12,13

```
interface GigabitEthernet0/1
  switchport mode trunk
  switchport trunk allowed vlan 10-12
!
interface GigabitEthernet0/4
  switchport access vlan 13
  switchport mode access
```

Switch B
Vlan 10,11,12,13

```
interface GigabitEthernet0/1
switchport mode trunk
!
interface GigabitEthernet0/3
   switchport access vlan 13
   switchport mode access
```

Refer to the exhibit. A network administrator assumes a task to complete the connectivity between PC A and the File Server. Switch A and Switch B have been partially configured with VLANs 10, 11, 12, and 13.

What is the next step in the configuration?

A. Add PC A to VLAN 10 and the File Server to VLAN 11 for VLAN segmentation.

B. Add VLAN 13 to the trunk links on Switch A and Switch B for VLAN propagation.

C. Add a router on a stick between Switch A and Switch B allowing for Inter-VLAN routing.

D. Add PC A to the same subnet as the File Server allowing for intra-VLAN communication.

118) R1 has learned route 192.168.12.0/24 via IS-IS, OSPF, RIP, and Internal EIGRP. Under normal operating conditions, which routing protocol is installed in the routing table?

A. IS-IS

B. Internal EIGRP

C. RIP

D. OSPF

119) A user configured OSPF in a single area between two routers. A serial interface connecting R1 and R2 is running encapsulation PPP. By default, which OSPF network type is seen on this interface when the user types show ip ospf interface on R1 or R2?

A. nonbroadcast.

B. point-to-point.

C. point-to-multipoint.

D. broadcast.

120) Which MAC address is recognized as a VRRP virtual address?

A. 0000.5E00.010a

B. 0005.3709.8968

C. 0000.0C07.AC99

D. 0007.C070.AB01

Answers & Explanation:

1) DE

C. to obtain VLAN information from directly connected switches - You can get the Native VLAN.

D. to verify Layer 2 connectivity between two devices when Layer 3 fails - Can get information even without L3.

E. to obtain the IP address of a connected device in order to telnet to the device - You can get the Management Address of a Switch.

2) CE

3) BDE

To communicate between two different VLANs we need to use a Layer 3 device like router or Layer 3 switch -> B is correct.

VLANs don't affect the number of collision domains, they are the same -> C is not correct. Typically, VLANs increase the number of broadcast domains.

We must use a different network (or sub-network) for each VLAN. For example, we can use 192.168.1.0/24 for VLAN 1, 192.168.2.0/24 for VLAN 2 -> D is correct.

A switch maintains a separate bridging table for each VLAN so that it can send frame to ports on the same VLAN only. For example, if a PC in VLAN 2 sends a frame then the switch look-ups its bridging table and only sends frame out of its ports which belong to VLAN 2 (it also sends this frame on trunk ports) -> E is correct.

A is wrong because there is always the default VLAN1.

4) A

Different VLANs can't communicate with each other, they can communicate with the help of Layer3 router. Hence, it is needed to connect a router to a switch, then make the sub-interface on the router to connect to the switch, establishing Trunking links to achieve communications of devices which belong to different VLANs.

5) B

LLDP is for support with non-Cisco devices, runs on the data link layer, and lldp timer has a configurable range from 5 to 65534 sec, commands configured only from conf t.

C affirms that the frequency value is a fixed value, but is not true. It can be modified.

6) C

C. send LWAPP packets to access points.

Lightweight APs (LAPs) is devices require no initial configuration. LAPs use the Lightweight Access Point Protocol (LWAPP) to communicate with a WLAN controller (WLC), as shown in the below figure. Controller-based APs are useful in situations where many APs are required in the network. As more APs are added, each AP is automatically configured and managed by the WLC.

7) A

4.1 Web proxy

Caching should be enabled in the web proxy configuration in order to save bandwidth and boost performance. This is becoming less important as the percentage of HTTPS traffic increases because the WSA does not by default cache HTTPS transactions. If the proxy is deployed to serve only explicit clients, forward mode should be specified in order to reject any traffic that isn't specifically destined for the proxy service. This reduces attack surface in the appliance and follows a good security principle: If you don't need it, turn it off.

Reference:

https://www.cisco.com/c/en/us/products/collateral/security/web-security-appliance/guide-c07-742373.html

8) B

The question asked "root port", so B is correct, the root port are ports with the lowest path cost to the root bridge.

Root Port selection is based on the port having lowest cost to the Root Bridge

(CAT1). For PVST (Per VLAN Spanning Tree) path cost will depend on bandwidth of links and cost value is as shown below for most commonly used links.

STP root port election.

Lowest root cost.

Lowest neighbor bridge ID.

Lowest neighbor port id.

Reference:

https://mrncciew.com/2013/07/07/stp-root-port-selection/

9) A

You can only create, add, delete edit vlan in server and transparent mode, you won't be able to create, delete vlan in client mode.

Switch(config)#vtp mode client

Setting device to VTP CLIENT mode.

Switch(config)#vla

Switch(config)#vlan 20

VTP VLAN configuration not allowed when device is in CLIENT mode.

10) AE

1. Spanning tree enabled protocol rstp (mode is Rapid PVST+)

2. Port 1 (FastEthernet 2/1) = root port is FastEthernet 2/1

11) A

Key is multi-vendor--lldp. cdp is cisco only.

12) B

Authentication, Identify users.

Authorization, access control.

Accounting, track user services.

13) B

"RADIUS combines authentication and authorization. The access-accept packets sent by the RADIUS server to the client contain authorization information. This makes it difficult to decouple authentication and authorization.

TACACS+ uses the AAA architecture, which separates AAA. This allows separate authentication solutions that can still use TACACS+ for authorization and accounting. For example, with TACACS+, it is possible to use Kerberos authentication and TACACS+ authorization and accounting."

Reference:
https://www.cisco.com/c/en/us/support/docs/security-vpn/remote-authentication-dial-user-service-radius/13838-10.html

14) A

"In local mode, an AP creates two CAPWAP tunnels to the WLC. One is for management; the other is data traffic. This behavior is known as "centrally switched" because the data traffic is switched(bridged) from the ap to the controller where it is then routed by some routing device."

Reference:

https://community.cisco.com/t5/wireless-and-mobility/what-s-the-difference-between-local-mode-and-flex-connect-mode/td-p/2532657

15) DE

Down/Down can be on account of phy problem: no cable attached, sw on other side shutdown, sw powered off, device speed mis match.

16) D

"When you enable LAG, only one functional physical port is needed for the controller to pass client traffic."

Reference:

https://www.cisco.com/c/en/us/td/docs/wireless/controller/8-2/config-guide/b_cg82/b_cg82_chapter_010101011.html

17) DE

To use SSH in Cisco Router.

01. IOS image must a k9(Crypto) image.

02. Configure DNS domain for the router (eg: ip domain-name R1.Contoso.lk).

Reference:

https://www.cisco.com/c/en/us/support/docs/security-vpn/secure-shell-ssh/4145-ssh.html

18) D

If neither the enable password command nor the enable secret command is configured, and if there is a line password configured for the console, the console line password serves as the enable password for all VTY sessions -> The "enable secret" will be used first if available, then "enable password" and line password.

If you set both enable password and enable secret. You will need to use the enable secret password to enter privileged mode.

19) D

Reference:

https://www.cisco.com/c/en/us/td/docs/switches/lan/catalyst4000/8-2glx/configuration/guide/stp_enha.html#:~:text=PortFast%20causes%20a%20switch%20or%20trunk%20port%20to%20enter%20the%20spanning%20tree%20forwarding%20state%20immediately%2C%20bypassing%20the%20listening%20and%20learning%20states.

20) B

You can protect communication with the GUI by enabling HTTPS. HTTPS protects

HTTP browser sessions by using the Secure Sockets Layer (SSL) protocol.

When you enable HTTPS, the controller generates its own local web administration SSL certificate and automatically applies it to the GUI. You also have the option of downloading an externally generated certificate.

This one is self-explaining - web(http) GUI + SSL = HTTPS

Reference:

https://www.cisco.com/c/en/us/td/docs/wireless/controller/8-0/configuration-guide/b_cg80/b_cg80_chapter_011.html

21) B

VLAN trunking offers two options, ISL and 802.1Q. ISL is Cisco proprietary while 802.1Q is standards based and supported by multiple vendors.

22) B

Command: switchport mode dynamic desirable, which asks the switch to both negotiate as well as to begin the negotiation process, rather than waiting on another device.

Reference:

https://www.ciscopress.com/articles/article.asp?p=2181837&seqNum=8#:~:text=switchport%20mode%20dynamic%20auto%3A%20Makes,to%

20trunk%20or%20desirable%20mode.&text=switchport%20mode%20dynamic%20desirable%3A%20Makes,link%20to%20a%20trunk%20link

23) C

22hex= 2*16^1+2*16^0=32+2=32 while 1D=1*16^1+13*16^0=16+13=29

It's the switch with the lowest MAC address.

24) C

The point here is to follow the rules. This is how the protocol works according to the rules I think it's true.

Dynamic auto + Dynamic desirable

Trunk + Trunk

Access + Access

switchport mode dynamic auto –

This is a default mode on the older CISCO switches. This mode makes the interface able to convert to a trunk link. The interface will become a trunk link if the neighboring interface is set to trunk or desirable mode. If both switches interface mode is auto, then the trunk will not be formed.

switchport mode dynamic desirable –

By this mode, the interface will actively attempt to convert the link into a trunk link. The interface will become a trunk port if the neighboring interface is set to trunk, desirable or auto.

Reference:

https://www.geeksforgeeks.org/dynamic-trunking-protocol-dtp/

25) B

26) A

27) C

From Cisco Press book 31 Days Before Your CCNA Exam:

"The network administrator wants to ensure that S1 is always the root bridge (...). The following commands achieve this objective:

S1(config)# spanning-tree vlan 1 root primary

The 'primary' keyword automatically sets the priority to 24576 or to the next 4096 increment value below the lowest bridge priority detected on the network."

This suggests to me whenever a new root bridge election is held, SW1 will update its priority so as to be the lowest.

28) A

Key Word is "passively" - so its Auto.

29) B

AS SWITCH KNOW DST, SO IT WILL REGISTER SRC IN CAM TABLE AND PASS THE DATA TO DST AS IT IS REGISTERED ALREADY IN CAM TABLE.

30) A

because let's say you wanted to configure the port as a management port, you would want to configure that interface first before the voice vlan.

31) A

if you put a switch with higher revision number will break up the database of the other switches, if you put a switch with lower revision number, it will update the database according with the other switches.

32) B

A. is a WIFI extension protocol.

C. is a means of bypassing 802.1x which is the opposite of what we want.

D. is when an attacker uses the same IP as the client. But the question states client devices as a given.

33) B

PoE switches support Cisco pre-standard PD detection mechanisms, and any Standards based compliant PDs. Most Cisco made PDs, pre-standard or standard, support Cisco Discovery Protocol (CDP). Once power is applied to a port that contains a pre-standard or standard Cisco PD, CDP is used in order to determine the actual power requirement, and the system power budget is adjusted accordingly.

34) D

802.11w PMF with protection and validation via secure hash to verify signed frames with MIC IE from a BSSID in the network. The secure pmf command is used together with the association-comeback time to configure a portion of this setup. In addition, helps more with capwap debugging for Cisco proprietary CCX/MFP messages between controller, APs, and devices. This method is supported on the newer WLCs.

Reference:

https://www.cisco.com/c/en/us/support/docs/smb/wireless/cisco-small-business-wireless-access-points/smb5442-frequently-asked-questions-about-management-frame-protection.html#q3

35) C

36) D

The switchport trunk native vlan command specifies the native (untagged) VLAN for a Layer 2 interface operating in trunk mode on a Cisco IOS device. This command only takes effect for interfaces that are operating in trunk mode.

untagged traffic goes through the native vlan.

37) CD

• Interfaces with portfast enabled that come up will go to forwarding mode immediately, the interface will skip the listening and learning state.

• A switch will never generate a topology change notification for an interface that has portfast enabled.

Reference:

https://networklessons.com/switching/cisc o-portfast-configuration

38) B

Portfast causes a switch or trunk port to enter the spanning tree forwarding state immediately, bypassing the listening and learning states.

39) B

The Switch looks at the Destination MAC for a matching address in its CAM table, not the source address. If the destination address does not exist in the CAM table the Switch forwards the packet out all ports "EXCEPT" the source port.

If it looks at the Source address it would just send it back the same port it came in on.

40) B

41) A

42) C

The switchport trunk allowed vlan command is used to specify the list of VLANs that are allowed on a trunk port. When a Layer 2 interface on a Cisco IOS device is configured to operate in trunk mode, the default setting is for the interface to carry all of the VLANs defined on the switch.

43) C

44) C

45) C

The normal or default MTU size typically used is 1500 bytes.

46) A

View Making Forwarding Decisions on:

https://www.cisco.com/c/en/us/support/d
ocs/ip/enhanced-interior-gateway-routing-
protocol-eigrp/8651-21.html

47) C

48) A

Reference:

https://www.cisco.com/c/en/us/support/d
ocs/ip/enhanced-interior-gateway-routing-
protocol-eigrp/16406-eigrp-toc.html#anc6

49) C

This one stumped me because I figured
192.168.1.1 would be the destination
address, but it should be the next hop
address.

50) B

Network 10.10.1.20 /30

host range 10.10.1.21 - 10.10.1.22

51) D

C is wrong since 192.168.12.16 is outside the host address range; therefore, a mask of 255.255.255.224 is able to route traffic properly with RIP /27

52) AC

Floating static routes are static routes that have an administrative distance greater than the administrative distance of dynamic routes. Administrative distances can be configured on a static route so that the static route is less desirable than a dynamic route. In this manner, the static route is not used when the dynamic route is available. However, if the dynamic route is lost, the static route can take over, and traffic can be sent through this alternate route. If this alternate route is provided using a DDR interface, then that interface can be used as a backup mechanism.

Used when primary route is Not available.

53) B

1. Longest Prefix

2. Administrative distance

3. Metric

Reference:

https://packetlife.net/blog/2010/aug/16/route-preference/

54) AD

Because EIGRP and OSPH has shortest admin. Distance

55) B

First, we need to check routing table to find out which network 10.10.13.165 IP address belongs to.

If we check routing table, 10.10.13.160/29 IP address/Mask combination covers the following IP addresses: 10.10.13.160 (network address), 10.10.13.161, 10.10.13.162, 10.10.13.163, 10.10.13.164, 10.10.13.165, 10.10.13.166, 10.10.13.167 (Broadcast address). Since the address to go is 10.10.13.165, the network it is in is 10.10.13.160/29.

But, in order to go 10.10.13.160/29 network, we need to pass from 10.10.10.5 next hop address. The question asks us which router has that address. In order to find it, we need to look at question. We see many 10.10.10.X/30 networks. If we analyze 10.10.10.4/30, we see that it covers 10.10.10.4 (network address), 10.10.10.5, 10.10.10.6 and 10.10.10.7(broadcast address) addresses. So 10.10.10.5 address belongs to 10.10.10.4/30 network which is between router1 and router3. So, the answer is Router3.

56) C

Route Preference:

1. Longest Prefix

2. Administrative Distance

3. Metric

In this specific question, the first option is: Administrative Distance.

57) AE

https://www.pearsonitcertification.com/articles/article.aspx?p=1868078#:~:text=2,area%20area-id

https://www.cisco.com/c/en/us/td/docs/ios-xml/ios/iproute_ospf/configuration/xe-3e/iro-xe-3e-book/iro-mode-ospfv2.pdf

https://www.ietf.org/rfc/rfc2328.txt#:~:text=Area%20ID%0A%20%20%20%20%20%20%20%20%20%20%20The%20OSPF%20ar

ea%20that%20the%20packet%20is%20bein
g%20sent%20into

58) B

For a Router on a stick, you need to:

1. create a sub-interface.

2. encapsulate dot1q with the VLAN ID.

3. Assign an IP address.

59) C

OSPF uses the following criteria to select the router ID:

1. Manual configuration of the router ID (via the "router-id x.x.x.x" command under OSPF router configuration mode).

2. Highest IP address on a loopback interface.

3. Highest IP address on a non-loopback and active (no shutdown) interface.

60) CE

It is asking the config on NY router.

ipv6 [loopback network] [serial interface IP]

IPv6: /128 provides a single IPv6 address.

61) C

The default hello time is 10 seconds which causes a mismatch.

62) D

default route is correct. 0.0.0.0/0 means when there is no any match in the routing table e.g. for www.google.com, that traffic must use the specified next hope/path (10.10.10.18). That's the way since we don't know the destination so the next hop/router will search the destination from neighboring routers up to the tear 1 if it's really available.

63) B

For internet traffic... the destination IP's can vary. Hence in this topology, it is using the default gateway 0.0.0.0. Path selection does not meet any other criteria so it has to use gateway of last resort.

64) C

OSPF uses cost to make routing decisions.

65) D

By default, IOS considers static routes better than OSPF-learned routes. By default, IOS gives static routes an administrative distance of 1 A floating static route floats or moves into and out of the IP routing table depending on whether the better (lower) administrative distance route learned by the routing protocol happens to exist currently.

66) C

A is wrong because default and designated routers are in use.

B is obviously wrong.

D is wrong, the neighbor count is 3.

C is correct, the default timers in broadcast networks (ethernet) are 10 seconds hello and 4*hello for the dead timer.

67) C

The Broadcast network type is the default for an OSPF enabled ethernet interface (while Point-to-Point is the default OSPF network type for Serial interface with HDLC and PPP encapsulation.

68) C

When IOS must choose between routes learned using different routing protocols, IOS uses a concept called administrative distance. Administrative distance is a number that denotes how believable an entire routing protocol is on a single router. The lower the number, the better

The AD is a rating of trust when multiple routes exist to the same destination.

Administrative distance is the feature used by routers to select the best path when there are two or more different routes to the same destination from different routing protocols. Administrative distance defines the reliability of a routing protocol.

69) B

Admin Distance:

Connected.................0

Static.........................1

EIGRP Summary......5 (This occurs only on the router where the summary was generated)

eBGP.........................20

Internal EIGRP.........90

OSPF.........................110

IS-IS...........................115

RIP.............................120

External EIGRP.......170

iBGP.......................200

NHRP.....................250 (You'll typically only when using phase 3 DMVPN)

Reference:

https://networktechstudy.com/home/learning-ospf-path-selection

70) D

Because when new route is learned by R1 it will be added to its routing table via Gi0/1 But the previous still stays in the routing table which is learned via Gi0/0 (ospf)

Hence, we have two paths to reach 10.10.13.0/25

Cisco plays with words, read carefully.

C is wrong because they used the word updated and not added. Updated means previous route is removed.

Which is not true, it stays in the table.

The AD of eBGP (20) is smaller than that of OSPF (110) so the route to 10.10.13.0/25 will be updated as being learned from the new BGP path.

71) BD

The reported distance (or advertised distance) is the cost from the neighbor to the destination. It is calculated from the router advertising the route to the network. For example in the topology below, suppose router A & B are exchanging their routing tables for the first time. Router B says λ€Hey, the best metric (cost) from me to IOWA is 50 and the metric from you to IOWA is 90λ€ and advertises it to router A. Router A considers the first metric (50) as the Advertised distance. The second metric (90), which is from NEVADA to IOWA (through IDAHO), is called the Feasible distance.

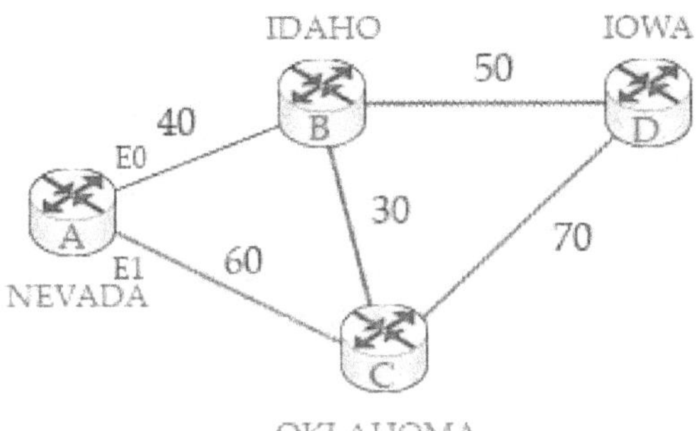

The reported distance is calculated in the same way of calculating the metric. By default (K1 = 1, K2 = 0, K3 = 1, K4 = 0, K5 = 0), the metric is calculated as follows:

$$metric = \left[\frac{10{,}000{,}000}{slowest\,bandwidth[in\,kbps]} + \frac{sum\,of\,delay[in\,\mu sec]}{10}\right] * 256$$

Feasible successor is the backup route. To be a feasible successor, the route must have an Advertised distance (AD) less than the Feasible distance (FD) of the current successor route.
Feasible distance (FD): The sum of the AD plus the cost between the local router and the next-hop router. The router must calculate the FD of all paths to choose the

best path to put into the routing table. Note: Although the new CCNA exam does not have EIGRP topic but you should learn the basic knowledge of this routing protocol.

72) D

Router2 does not have an entry for the subnet 10.10.13.128/25. It only has an entry for 10.10.13.0/25, which ranges from 10.10.13.0 to 10.10.13.127.

73) AE

Hot Standby Router Protocol (HSRP) A Cisco proprietary protocol that allows two (or more) routers to share the duties of being the default router on a subnet, with an active/standby model, with one router acting as the default router and the other sitting by waiting to take over that role if the first router fails

HSRP

Protocol Cisco proprietary

"Number of groups" 16 groups maximum

Active/Standby "1 active, 1 standby and multiple candidates."

"Virtual IPAddress" "Different from real IP addresses on interfaces"

Multicast address 224.0.0.2

Tracking Interfaces or Objects

HSRP virtual Mac address will start with 0000.0c07.acXX

07.ac is the hexadecimal conversion of the HSRP group Id.

XX is Group number

virtual Mac for hsrp group 2 = 0000.0c07.ac02

virtual Mac for hsrp group12 = 0000.0c07.ac0C

74) AE

A is correct because it's asking for WHEN the link goes down. So, you still need to configure the primary link.

E is correct because Ipv6 route 2000::1/128 2023::3 5 = NY to Washington (backup route hence AD = 5).

Seems this BACKUP-route via NY to Washington is the only link requiring setup in real life - to answer the Q.

Floating static routes are static routes that have an administrative distance greater than the administrative distance (AD) of another static route or dynamic routes.

By default, a static route has an AD of 1 then floating static route must have the AD greater than 1. Floating static route has a manually configured administrative distance greater than that of the primary route and therefore would not be in the routing table until the primary route fails.

75) B

This virtual IP address is in the same subnet as the interface IP address, but it is a different IP address. The router then automatically creates the virtual MAC address. All the cooperating HSRP routers know these virtual addresses, but only the HSRP active router uses these addresses at any one point in time.

The virtual router is responsible for host communications such as an ARP request for the host's default gateway. Technically, this is served by the active router since it is hosting the virtual router. However, it is the virtual router's IP address and MAC address that are used for outgoing packets.

Reference:

https://www.cisco.com/c/en/us/td/docs/ios-xml/ios/ipapp_fhrp/configuration/xe-16/fhp-xe-16-book/fhp-hsrp-mgo.html

76) D

Pay attention to the statement: "establishes the OSPF neighbor relationship without forming an adjacency".

These two conditions (1) NO Neighbor Missing AND (2) no adjacency occurs only in two situations:

1) Neighboring interfaces with MTU mismatch.

2) Neighboring interfaces with OSPF network type mismatch.

OSPF doesn't use broadcast so the network type as to change.

also, to form an adjacent the hello and dead timers must match, and we don't want that here.

Reference:

https://learning.oreilly.com/library/view/ccna-200-301-official/9780136755562/vol1_ch21.xhtml

77) A

Preemption is the technology that ask a HSRP enabled router to be primary every time it comes up even though backup router is acting as Primary currently. if Preemption not enabled, when primary router reloads then backup router becomes primary and does not become backup even though primary router comes up.

The "preempt" command enables the HSRP router with the highest priority to immediately become the active router.

78) D

On the contrary if the question is vrrp, command is:

show vrrp.

And for GLBP, show glbp.

79) B

Not A because question asks for Non default AD therefore, we use 5 as AD for static route and not 1 because Default AD for static route is 1.

The default AD of static route is 1 so we need to configure another number for the static route.

80) BE

Distance Vector - RIP & EIGRP

OSPF - Link State & IS IS

BGP - Path State

Reference:

https://packetlife.net/media/library/40/IOS
_Interior_Routing_Protocols.pdf

81) A

Once an OSPF Router ID selection is done, it remains there even if you remove it or configure another OSPF Router ID. So, the least disruptive way is to correct it using the command "clear ip ospf process".

It shouldn't be B (especially if you configured router-id x.x.x.x as indicated in problem statement). Clear ip ospf process temporarily restarts the neighbor relationships and there is disruption but my understanding it is only temporary. OSPF is self-healing with the hello packets.

So, the OSPF routers should reconverge.

82) D

show ip eigrp events

To display the Enhanced Interior Gateway Routing Protocol (EIGRP) event log, use the show ip eigrp events command in user EXEC or privileged EXEC mode.

Reference:

https://www.cisco.com/c/en/us/td/docs/ios-xml/ios/iproute_eigrp/command/ire-cr-book/ire-s1.html#wp3095206170

83) BC

E is not correct because is not static is learned via external eigrb.

In in this routing table, I do not see:

S* 0.0.0.0/0 [1/0] via 10.85.33.14

This means we DO NOT have a static default route configured.

Ps. Reference the routing tables in the exhibits from Q's 159 and 166 to see what a static default route looks like.

84) BC

Exterior Gateway Protocols (EGP): Used for routing between autonomous systems. It is also referred to as inter-AS routing. Service providers and large companies may interconnect using an EGP. The Border Gateway Protocol (BGP) is the only currently viable EGP and is the official routing protocol used by the Internet.

NOTE

Because BGP is the only EGP available, the term EGP is rarely used; instead, most engineers simply refer to BGP.

Reference:

https://www.ciscopress.com/articles/article.asp?p=2180210&seqNum=7

85) BC

B and C represent the same thing, i.e., by changing variance to 2 allows value to be same (2*3072=6144) which is C & B states to change the configuration to achieve same feasible distance which is if variance 2 is given both will have the same feasible distance.

Reference:

https://www.cisco.com/c/en/us/support/docs/ip/enhanced-interior-gateway-routing-protocol-eigrp/13677-19.html#topic1

86) DE

87) ABE

Hierarchical design of OSPF (basically means that you can separate the larger internetwork into smaller internetworks called areas) helps us create a network with all features listed above (decrease routing overhead, speed up convergence, confine network instability to single areas of the network).

88) A

No route to that destination could be found in the table so the router sends the packets to the default route.

89) D

No AD needed. Rule most specified Prefix you need. The AD=90.

90) A

D is not correct because the .33 is the first available host in the network and .32 is the network itself.

91) B

longest prefix match, /32

EIGRP AD=90

92) B

Q. If there is no priority configured for a standby group, what determines which router is active?

A. The priority field is used to elect the active router and the standby router for the specific group. In the case of an equal priority, the router with the highest IP address for the respective group is elected as active. Furthermore, if there are more than two routers in the group, the second highest IP address determines the standby router and the other router/routers are in the listen state.

93) ACD

auto summary uses "classful boundary"

- 10.4.3.0 with mask 255.0.0.0 gives 10.0.0.0

- 172.16.4.0 with mask 255.255.0.0 gives 172.16.0.0

- 192.168.2.0 with mask 255.255.255.0 gives 192.168.2.0

Classless routing in EIGRP auto summary so

Class A 10.0.0.0 / 8

Class B 172.16.0.0 /16

Class C 192.168.x.0 /24

94) A

Simply because that will be the default behavior routers would follow in the event all other routers in the HSRP group fail, then it would not keep attributes such as priority or preemption. What preemption does in summary is to make sure that the configured Priority on all routers within the same HSRP group is always respected. That is, if R1 is configured on the HSRP group with a priority of 150 but he stands as active since all other routers currently subscribed to that group have a priority 150, then will router will preempt the current active router and will take over hence becoming the new active router.

With preemption disabled, the new router does not preempt the current active router, unless routers in the group have to renegotiate their roles based on each router's priority at the time of negotiation.

95) AB

96) C

Router has pointed default router to 192.168.4.1 and this subnet is connected via serial 2 interface. Router does not have router for the 192.0.2.156. So, it will use the default gateway 192.168.4.1. A default route identifies the gateway IP address to which the router sends all IP packets for which it does not have a learned or static route.

97) ACE

The OSPF protocol is based on link-state technology, which is a departure from the Bellman-Ford vector-based algorithms used in traditional Internet routing protocols such as RIP. OSPF has introduced new concepts such as authentication of routing updates, Variable Length Subnet Masks (VLSM), route summarization, and so forth.

OSPF uses flooding to exchange link-state updates between routers. Any change in routing information is flooded to all routers in the network. Areas are introduced to put a boundary on the explosion of link-state updates. Flooding and calculation of the Dijkstra algorithm on a router is limited to changes within an area.

98) A

Because "ospf fails to START" and the only must-have requirements for ist to start are matching area IDs and hello/dead timers.

99) D

The "show ip ospf database" command displays the link states. Here is an example:

Here is the lsa database on R2.

R2#show ip ospf database -

OSPF Router with ID (2.2.2.2) (Process ID 1)

Router Link States (Area 0)

Link ID ADV Router Age Seq# Checksum Link count2.2.2.2   2.2.2.2   793   0x80000003 0x004F85   210.4.4.4   10.4.4.4   776 0x80000004 0x005643 1111.111.111.111

111.111.111.111   755   0x80000005 0x0059CA   2133.133.133.133 133.133.133.133   775   0x80000005 0x00B5B1 2 Net Link States (Area 0)

Link   ID   ADV   Router   Age   Seq# Checksum10.1.1.1   111.111.111.111   794 0x80000001   0x001E8B10.2.2.3 133.133.133.133   812   0x80000001 0x004BA910.4.4.1

111.111.111.111   755   0x80000001 0x007F1610.4.4.3   133.133.133.133   775 0x80000001 0x00C31F

100) BCD

OSPF will match IP addresses based on 192.168.12.64 0.0.0.63.

11000000.10101000.00001100.01000000
=> 192.168.12.64

00000000.00000000.00000000.00111111
=> 0.0.0.63

Matches will be made on the IP only for the 1's not 0's above. We can invert the bits to make it more familiar as a network mask. This becomes:

11000000.10101000.00001100.01000000
=> 192.168.12.64

11111111.11111111.11111111.11000000
=> /26 or 255.255.255.192

This therefore gives a match of IPs in the network 192.168.12.64 (the next network is 192.168.12.128) so broadcast is 192.168.12.127 and usable IPs are .65 to 126.

We now match IPs in this range which are:

FastEthernet0/1 (192.168.12.65) - ANSWER B

Serial0/0 (192.168.12.121) - ANSWER C

Serial0/1/102 (192.168.12.125) - ANSWER D

If you are having problems understanding this one the key to write out 0.0.0.63 in binary and then invert the bits.

The "network 192.168.12.64 0.0.0.63 equals to network 192.168.12.64/26. This network has:

▻ Increment: 64 (/26= 1111 1111.1111 1111.1111 1111.1100 0000) + Network address:

192.168.12.64

▻ Broadcast address: 192.168.12.127

Therefore, all interface in the range of this network will join OSPF.

101) D

They list the routing protocols to throw you off. The question is actually testing your knowledge of VLAN routing.

Since all the same router (C-router) is the default gateway for all three VLANs, all traffic destined to a different VLA will be sent to the C-router. The C-router will have knowledge of all three networks since they will appear as directly connected in the routing table. Since the C-router already knows how to get to all three networks, no routing protocols need to be configured.

102) C

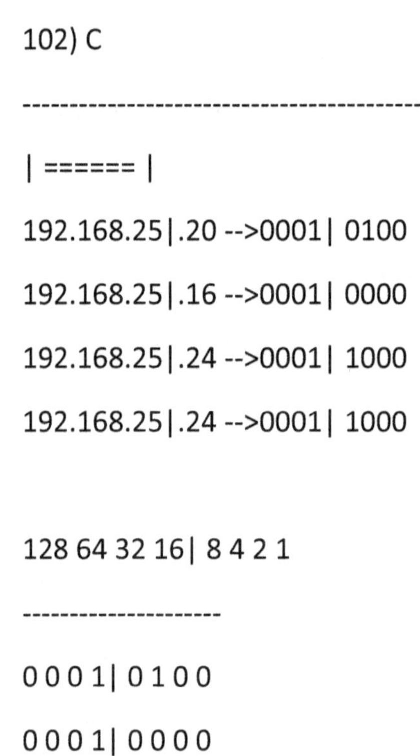

0 0 0 1| 1 0 0 0

192.168.25.16/28 == 255.255.255.240

==>192.168.25.16 /255.255.255.240

The binary version of 20 is 10100.

The binary version of 16 is 10000.

The binary version of 24 is 11000.

The binary version of 28 is 11100.

The subnet mask is /28. The mask is 255.255.255.240.

Note:

From the output above, EIGRP learned 4 routes and we need to find out the summary of them:

☞ 192.168.25.16

192.168.25.20

☞ 192.168.25.24

192.168.25.28

-> The increment should be 28 ?16 = 12 but 12 is not an exponentiation of 2; so, we must choose 16 (24). Therefore, the subnet mask is /28 (=1111 1111.1111

1111.1111 1111.11110000) = 255.255.255.240.

So, the best answer is 192.168.25.16 255.255.255.240.

103) C

If router ID is not manually setup, the highest loopback IP is selected and if there is no loopback, highest IP from the interface IPs is selected.

The highest IP address of all loopback interfaces will be chosen -> Loopback 0 will be chosen as the router ID.

104) A

This question is to examine the understanding of the interaction between

EIGRP routers. The following information must be matched so as to create neighborhood. EIGRP routers to establish, must match the following information:

1. AS Number.

2. K value.

105) D

In OSPF, the hello and dead intervals must match and here we can see the hello interval is set to 5 on R1 and 10 on R2. The dead interval is also set to 20 on R1 but it is 40 on R2.

By the way, the interfaces on both routers have the same IP address.

106) BC

OSPF uses the following criteria to select the router ID:

1. Manual configuration of the router ID (via the "router-id x.x.x.x" command under OSPF router configuration mode).

2. Highest IP address on a loopback interface.

3. Highest IP address on a non-loopback and active (no shutdown) interface.

With OSPF, the loopback interface is useful because it is an interface with an IP address which never goes down (stability).

107) C

A router ID is determined in the following order:

1. using the router-id command under the OSPF process to statically configure the router ID.

2. using the highest IP address of the router's loopback interfaces.

3. using the highest IP address of the router's active physical interfaces.

108) AC

B: wrong, by default 40 seconds.

D: wrong, not only between neighboring interfaces.

E: wrong, designated router is not elected based on its hello-response time, but on its priority / router ID.

F: wrong, multicast and not broadcast is used for hello packets.

The DEAD timer is 40 sec by default, the hello timer is 10 sec for ethernet networks.

109) AB

Exactly one active router: Only one Active Router per HSRP group will be elected based on highest priority. In case of equal priority, Highest IP address will be elected as Active Router.

One or more standby routers: There can be one or more Standby Routers.

110) CE

Adjacencies are shown with (confg)# sh ip (ospf, eigrp) neighbor.

(This is hoping and assuming that you would not manually input the same admin distance as an existing protocol on a route).

111) B

Because the AD is 90.

112) AB

Timers match by default.

The process ID can be the same or not.

The router ID mustn't be the same.

113) D

It uses the default route since there is no entry for the destination address/subnet entry in the routine table.

There is no network in the routing table that includes 172.16.0.14 in its IP range, so the router needs to default to the gateway of last resort, which in this case is the serial 0/1/0 interface with the next-hop IP address 209.165.200.246.

114) D

172.16.3.14 routes to ospf route 172.16.3.0-16 /28

Routers prefer routes with the "longest match". Meaning the smallest prefix that contains the host's IP address. /28 is a longer match than /24.

115) A

Admin Distance:

Connected - 0

Static - 1

eBGP - 5

iEIGRP - 90

OSPF - 110

IS-IS - 115

RIP – 120

116) D

117) B

They are not on different subnets. Subnet 192.168.0.0 /23 has 2^9 = 512 hosts, which spans an IP range of 192.168.0.0 - 192.168.1.255. Addresses 192.168.0.10 and 192.168.1.20 are on the same range and their respective interfaces are on the same VLAN. The only problem here is that the trunk link on Switch A doesn't allow VLAN 13.

118) B

With the same route (prefix), the router will choose the routing protocol with lowest Administrative Distance (AD) to install into the routing table. The AD of Internal EIGRP (90) is lowest so it would be chosen. The table below lists the ADs of popular routing protocols.

Route Source	Administrative Distance
Directly Connected	0
Static	1
EIGRP	90
EIGRP Summary route	5
OSPF	110
RIP	120

Note: The AD of IS-IS is 115. The "EIGRP" in the table above is "Internal EIGRP". The AD of "External EIGRP" is 170. An EIGRP external route is a route that was redistributed into EIGRP.

119) B

Broadcast default for Ethernet, Point to Point default for serial.

The default OSPF network type for HDLC and PPP on Serial link is point-to-point (while the default OSPF network type for Ethernet link is Broadcast).

120) A

1 VRRP over Ethernet. Over Ethernet, VRRP routers use a common MAC address of the format 00:00:5E: 00:01:XX. The first three octets are derived from the IANA's OUI. The next two octets (00:01) indicate the address block assigned to the VRRP protocol by IANA.

Virtual MAC address: A virtual MAC address is automatically generated by taking the last 8 bytes as the VRRP group number in hexadecimal. In VRRP, Mac address used is 0000.5e00.01xx. Here, xx is the VRRP group number in hexadecimal.

Reference:

https://www.geeksforgeeks.org/introduction-of-virtual-router-redundancy-protocol-vrrp-and-its-configuration/

GOOD

LUCK

www.ingramcontent.com/pod-product-compliance
Lightning Source LLC
Chambersburg PA
CBHW051947150726
47999CB00004B/1287